Aspects of Zaiwa Prosody

An Autosegmental Account

Summer Institute of Linguistics and
The University of Texas at Arlington
Publications in Linguistics

Publication 129

Publications in Linguistics is a series published jointly by the Summer Institute of Linguistics and the University of Texas at Arlington. The series is a venue for works covering a broad range of topics in linguistics, especially the analytical treatment of minority languages from all parts of the world. While most volumes are authored by members of the Institute, suitable works by others also form part of the series.

Series Editors

Donald A. Burquest
University of Texas
at Arlington

Mildred A. Larson
Summer Institute
of Linguistics

Volume Editor

Bonnie Brown
Rhonda L. Hartell

Production Staff

Bonnie Brown, Managing Editor
Laurie Nelson, Production Manager
Karoline Fisher, Compositor
Hazel Shorey, Graphic Arts

Aspects of Zaiwa Prosody

Mark W. Wannemacher

A Publication of
The Summer Institute of Linguistics
and
The University of Texas at Arlington
1998

© 1998 by the Summer Institute of Linguistics, Inc.
Library of Congress Catalog No: 98–60951
ISBN: 1-55671-054-2
ISSN: 1040-0850

Printed in the United States of America
All Rights Reserved

08 07 06 05 04 03 02 01 00 99   10 9 8 7 6 5 4 3 2 1

No part of this publication may be reproduced, stored in a retrieval system, or transmitted in any form or by any means—electronic, mechanical, photocopy, recording, or otherwise—without the express permission of the Summer Institute of Linguistics, with the exception of brief excerpts in journal articles or reviews.

Copies of this and other publications of the Summer Institute of Linguistics may be obtained from

International Academic Bookstore
Summer Institute of Linguistics
7500 W. Camp Wisdom Rd.
Dallas, TX 75236-5699

Voice: 972-708-7404
Fax: 972-708-7433
Email: academic_books@sil.org
Internet: http://www.sil.org

Contents

1 Introduction 1
   1.1 Purpose of this study 1
   1.2 Historical, cultural, and geographic background of
       Zaiwa 2
   1.3 Linguistic classifications of Zaiwa 4
   1.4 General characteristics of Tibeto-Burman languages 8
   1.5 Methodology and analysis 8
   1.6 Overview of the primary research problems
       and organization of this study 9

2 Previous Studies of Zaiwa Phonology 11
   2.1 Syllable structure 12
   2.2 Consonant and consonant cluster inventory 13
   2.3 Phonological processes affecting consonants 14
   2.4 Vowel inventory 14
   2.5 Phonological processes affecting vowels 15
   2.6 Consonant and vowel distribution 15
   2.7 Tone 15
   2.8 Voice quality 17
   2.9 Discussion 18

3 Phonological Prerequisites to the Analysis and Representation of Zaiwa Phonology 19
   3.1 Overview of autosegmental phonology assumptions 19
   3.2 Overview of phonological features and feature geometry . . . 21
   3.3 Overview of underspecification theory 23
   3.4 Overview of pitch and voice quality production and interactions 23
      3.4.1 The anatomy and physiology of the larynx 24
      3.4.2 Pitch production 25
      3.4.3 The interaction of pitch with segments 26
      3.4.4 Voice quality production 31
      3.4.5 The interaction of pitch and voice quality 33

4 An Autosegmental Framework for the Analysis and Representation of Tone and Voice Quality in Zaiwa 37
   4.1 Prerequisites to tonal representation 38
      4.1.1 Contour and register tone 38
      4.1.2 Features included with tone 39
      4.1.3 Lexical and derived tone in Zaiwa 39
   4.2 The domains of tone and voice quality 41
   4.3 Previous representations of tone and voice quality 44
      4.3.1 The laryngeal feature system of Halle and Stevens . . . 45
      4.3.2 Laryngeal feature geometry proposed by Duanmu . . . 46
      4.3.3 Laryngeal feature geometry proposed by Ladefoged . . 48
      4.3.4 Tonal and laryngeal feature geometry proposed by Yip 49
   4.4 A framework for the autosegmental analysis and representation of tone and voice quality in Zaiwa 50
      4.4.1 Underspecification and feature geometry for the representation of tone and voice quality in Zaiwa 51
      4.4.2 The representation of lexical tone and voice quality in Zaiwa modal and tense voice syllables 54
      4.4.3 The representation of derived tone and lexical voice quality in Zaiwa modal and tense voice checked syllables 58

Contents vii

5 Aspects of Zaiwa Segmental Phonology 65
5.1 The phonological word 65
5.2 Syllable structure 66
5.2.1 A traditional approach to syllable structure 67
5.2.2 A moraic approach to syllable structure 70
5.2.3 Syllable onset and syllable weight 72
5.2.4 Zaiwa syllable distribution 74
5.2.5 Reduced syllables 75
5.3 Zaiwa consonants 79
5.3.1 Phonemic representation of consonants 79
5.3.2 Deaspiration or devoicing of plosives and affricates . . 80
5.4 Zaiwa vowels 83
5.4.1 Phonemic representation of vowels 84
5.4.2 Vowel shortening 84
5.5 Distribution of phonemes, tonemes, and voice quality 85

6 Zaiwa Suprasegmental Phonology 87
6.1 Introduction to Zaiwa tone 87
6.2 Tone in reduced syllables 89
6.3 Tonal processes in close juncture 91
6.3.1 Allotonic tonal processes 91
6.3.2 Tone sandhi 96
6.4 Tone in checked syllables 106
6.5 Tone contrasts 110
6.6 Low tone 111
6.7 Stress and tone 112
6.8 Voice quality 114
6.9 Conclusion 120

Appendix A: Further Details of Zaiwa Segmental Phonology . . . 123
A.1 Consonantal contrasts 123
A.2 Additional phonological processes affecting consonants . . 127
A.3 Vocalic contrasts 129
A.4 Additional phonological processes affecting vowels 132
A.5 Additional discussion on the distribution of phonemes . . . 139
A.6 Allophone statements 142

A.7 Morphophonemics 145

Appendix B: Distinctive Feature Charts 149

References 155

1
Introduction

1.1 Purpose of this study

The purpose of this study is to provide a generative and autosegmental phonological analysis of the Zaiwa language with emphasis on prosodic components. Three previous analyses of Zaiwa phonology (Burling 1967:16–19, Xu and Xu 1984:6–20, Yabu 1988:105–9) have covered the basic phonological features of the language, including its segments, tones, and voice quality, in varying degrees of explicitness. Burling provides a short description of segments, tones, and voice quality, but does not present an analysis. Xu and Xu have written the most extensive phonology to date and provide some analysis, including some tonal processes. The work differs from the other two in the way it relates phonetic forms to phonological contrasts.[1] Yabu provides a short description with a small amount of analysis in a structuralist framework. None of these analyses of Zaiwa present the material in a modern framework.

This study is to be regarded as a preliminary phonology of the Zaiwa language with a relatively complete treatment of all phonological aspects, concentrating especially on suprasegmental components. The generative/autosegmental framework employed incorporates feature geometry in a manner that shows the interaction of segmentals and suprasegmentals. I will be taking a stand on the syllable, segmental phonological processes, tone, tone change, tone and segment interaction,

---
[1] I would like to thank Henry and Florence Lau for their translation of the phonology section of Xu and Xu 1984.

and voice quality that draws on and, to some extent, elaborates current linguistic literature in the autosegmental tradition. It is my hope that this study will provide a basis for understanding the processes occurring in Zaiwa phonology and provide helpful insights into similar processes in other Tibeto-Burman languages.[2]

1.2 Historical, cultural, and geographic background of Zaiwa

Zaiwa [dzaiwa] is a language of about 100,000 speakers in the Northern Burmic branch[3] of the Tibeto-Burman language family. The name of the language varies depending on whether endonyms or exonyms are being used. Speakers of the language group refer to themselves as Zaiwa in all locations. In Myanmar (formerly Burma), the Jinghpaw use the term Atsi for the Zaiwa, and the Burmese use the term Zi (Bradley 1979:85). In China they are called Szi and are classified as a part of the Jingpo[4] Nationality, Zaiwa language.

The Zaiwa are one of several language groups which make up the Kachin sociocultural grouping.[5] The relationship is based on cultural similarities, historical contact, and intermarriage. There are many mixed

---

[2]I am grateful to the many individuals who helped make this book possible. Jerold Edmondson, David Silva, and Don Burquest were a great help in developing a framework for analysis and representation in the initial stages of the work. I would also like to thank Ken Gregerson and Fraser Bennett for improving on the initial presentation and offering sound suggestions for reworking various portions of the text. Any mistakes or inadequacies in presentation are fully the doing of the author.

The data for this work was collected while I was living in Chiang Mai, Thailand. I would like to thank Payap University for sponsoring my research in the country. None of the research could have been done without input from three patient Zaiwa speakers, Roi Seng, Lashan, and Tangun, to who I am grateful.

Special thanks goes to my wife, Leslie, and children, Jacob, Anna, and Nathan, whose patience, support, and encouragement made the task much easier. Final thanks goes to God, who enables the beauty of linguistic diversity and order in linguistic complexity.

[3]This classification follows Shafer's system as shown in (4). See §1.3 for other classifications.

[4]The Chinese literature transliterates Jinghpaw as Jingpo. Jinghpaw is the spelling used by the Jinghpaw themselves.

[5]The term Kachin can be used in two different senses. First, Kachin is the Burmese exonym [kətʃʰí] for the Jinghpaw language group, which is in a different linguistic branch of Tibeto-Burman than Zaiwa. Secondly, Kachin is used as an ethnonym encompassing as many as fourteen language groups spread across four major subfamilies of the Tibeto-Burman tree, the major ones being Jinghpaw, Rawang, Zaiwa, Lashi, Maru, Ngochang, and some of the Northern Burma Lisu. In this book, the term "Kachin" will be used as an ethnonym.

Introduction

villages, especially between the Zaiwa and Jinghpaw. Linguistically, however, Zaiwa is much closer to Burmese than to Jinghpaw.[6] The Zaiwa of Myanmar use the Jinghpaw language as their lingua franca and many can also speak Burmese. The Zaiwa in Yunnan tend to also speak Yunnanese Chinese, but not Jinghpaw.

The Zaiwa have traditionally been swidden agriculturists. The men fish, hunt, raise livestock, clear and burn fields, and maintain political and religious roles. Women plant and harvest crops, carry water, gather firewood, make clothes, and prepare food. Descent is traced patrilineally with each clan claiming a different remote ancestor as first descendent. Clan relationships among the Kachin groups override differences of language and local customs. The Zaiwa are organized politically according to the Gumsa[7] system of Kachin government. Each local Zaiwa group is under the authority of a chief. The Zaiwa are by tradition animists holding to both ancestral spirits and minor deities such as household guardians. Since the early 1900s, a large number of Zaiwa have become Christian, both Protestant and Catholic.

The majority of the Zaiwa (69,000) live in Yunnan province of southwest China along the border with Myanmar (Diehl 1992).

(1)   Mainland Southeast Asia and southern China

---

[6]An account for the close genetic affiliation of Zaiwa with Burmese has been recently suggested by Bradley (1993:173). He states that the Zaiwa and the Burmans lived together in the hills northeast of the plains of Upper Burma in the 9th century prior to the descent of the Burmans into central Burma.

[7]Gumsa is the term used for a political system intermediate between Jinghpaw democracy and aristocratic Shan ideals.

More specifically the Zaiwa reside in Luxi, Ruili, Longchuan, and Yingjiang counties of Dehong Dai-Jingpo Autonomous Prefecture in Yunnan province (Yabu 1988). The Zaiwa are classified as part of the Jingpo Nationality in China, one of fifty-five officially recognized ethnic minorities. Another 30,000 Zaiwa speakers are found in northeast Kachin state in northern Myanmar concentrated near Sadon along the border with China and in the cities of Myitkyina and Bhamo. There are also about three hundred Zaiwa near Kengtung in Shan state,[8] Myanmar, and a few are also found in Thailand in Kachin villages near Chiang Dao.

(2)   Locations of Zaiwa speakers from inset map in (1)

The Zaiwa have traditionally lived in rough, mountainous areas with intervening narrow valleys running north and south. Due to the tenuous political situation in Myanmar over the past forty years, many Zaiwa have migrated to the cities and gem-mining centers to escape the hardships of rural life.

1.3 Linguistic classifications of Zaiwa

The Zaiwa belong to the rich macrocosm of polyglot East and Southeast Asia. Indeed, Southeast Asia is home to three major linguistic families: Austro-Asiatic, Austro-Tai, and Sino-Tibetan. Benedict (1972) and Matisoff (1978) further divide Sino-Tibetan into the Sinitic (Chinese) and Tibeto-Karen language subgroupings as shown in (3). The Tibeto-Karen branch is divided again into Tibeto-Burman and Karen branches,

---

[8]The Zaiwa in Kengtung were apparently sent to the area as a gift and bodyguard for the marriage of a Shan Sawba and a Kachin princess.

Introduction

although there is some disagreement as to whether Tibeto-Burman and Karen form a joint group under Sino-Tibetan or are simply sister branches under Sino-Tibetan. Most linguists would agree that Tibeto-Burman is at some level a sub-branch of Sino-Tibetan.

(3) Classification of Tibeto-Burman under Sino-Tibetan

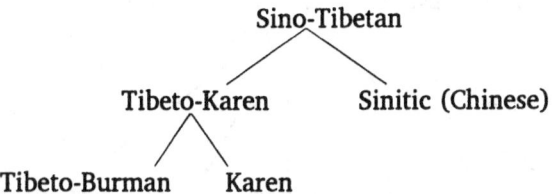

Zaiwa has been assigned several positions under Tibeto-Burman. Four major classifications are presented in (4)–(7), simplified by having only the nodes associated with Zaiwa[9] and other Kachin languages spelled out (Hale 1982).

(4) Position of Zaiwa (Atsi) in Tibeto-Burman (Shafer 1966)

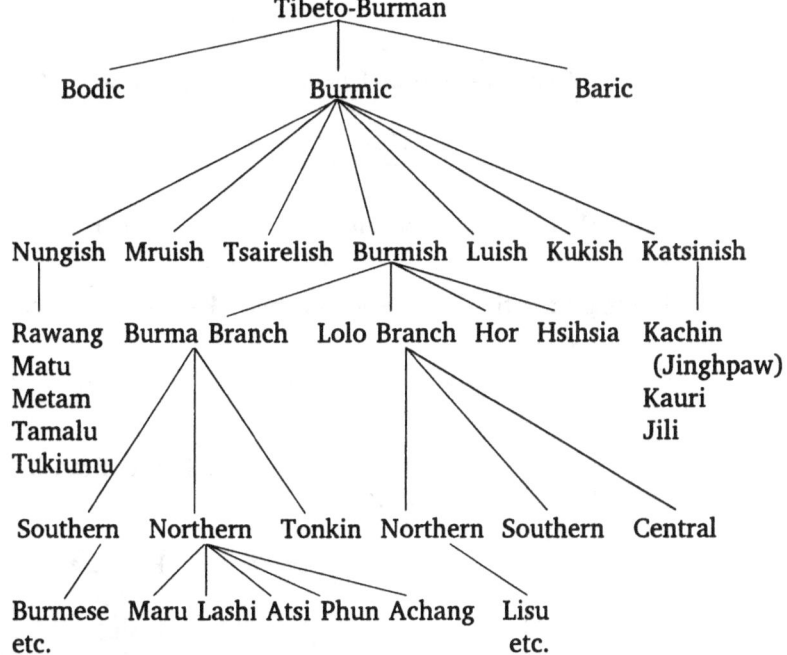

---

[9]In most classifications the authors have chosen to use the term Atsi instead of Zaiwa.

(5)   Position of Zaiwa (Atsi) in Tibeto-Burman (Benedict 1972)

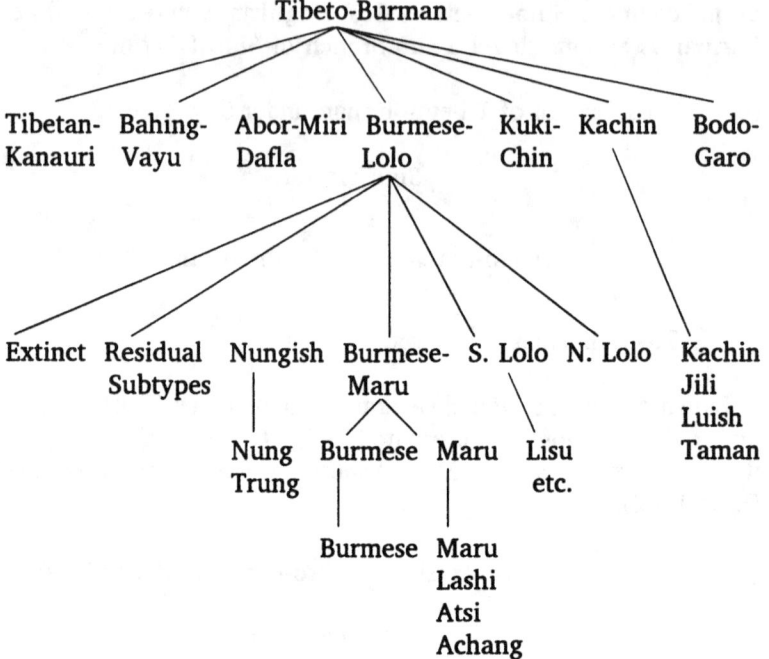

(6)   Position of Zaiwa (Atsi) in Tibeto-Burman (Egerod 1974)

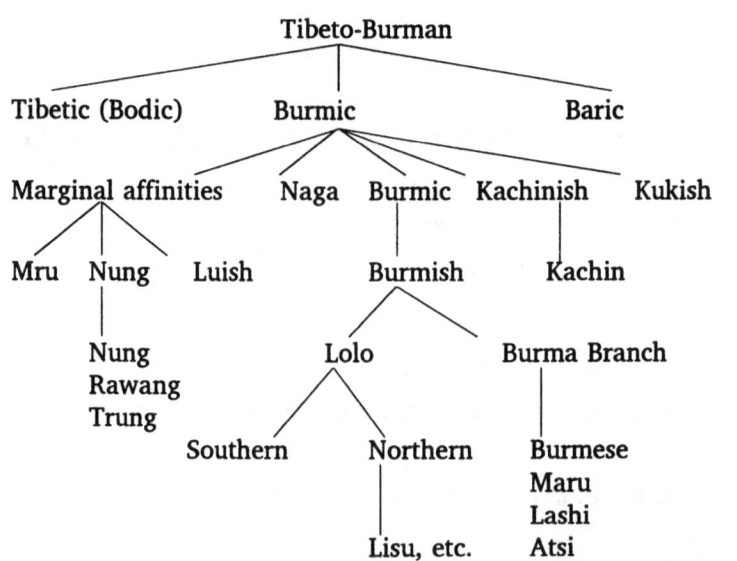

(7) Position of Zaiwa (Atsi) in Tibeto-Burman (Dai Qingxia 1993)

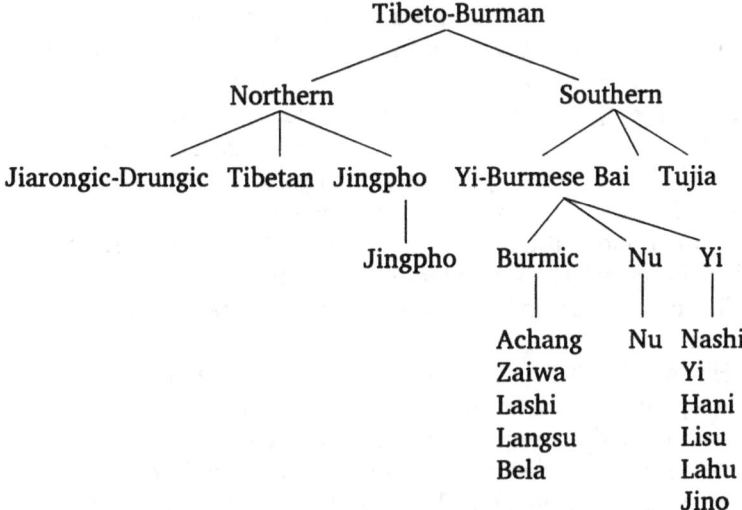

Most linguists use Shafer's classification of Zaiwa as a language in the Northern Burma branch of Tibeto-Burman. As indicated in the Stammbaum diagrams (4)–(7), Zaiwa is most closely related to Maru, Lashi, and Ngochang, and more distantly to Burmese.[10]

There is little difference between the Zaiwa spoken in Myanmar and that spoken in China, except for lexical borrowings.[11] The Zaiwa in China tend to borrow from Yunnanese Chinese, and the Zaiwa in Myanmar tend to borrow more from Jinghpaw, Burmese, and Shan. Zaiwa shows significantly more cognates with Jinghpaw than do other Kachin languages.[12] Zaiwa also shows an almost identical phonemic inventory with that of Jinghpaw. There are both high and vernacular (common) forms of speech in Zaiwa, a kind of diglossia. The data presented in this study will reflect only common forms.

---

[10]Other languages which may have close association with the Burmish languages are Moso (Naxi), Xixia, Tosu (Bradley 1979:12), Hpun, Kadu, Danu, Taungyo, Yaw (Bradley 1979:83), and Bela (Edmondson 1993). The details of their relationships still need to be worked out.

[11]I have collected data from Zaiwa speakers who originated from both China and Myanmar and compared the results. Preliminary comparison shows a high degree of cognate correspondence. This observation also agrees with Yabu who states, "The comparative study of the Atsi language of China and Burma mentions that there is little regional differentiation of this language and indicates that the Atsi language has maintained a high level of homogeneity" (1988:127).

[12]I compared the first four hundred words of the SIL Mainland SE Asia wordlist for Zaiwa and Jinghpaw, Myitkyina dialect. Zaiwa had seven percent obvious cognates or borrowings from Jinghpaw.

1.4 General characteristics of Tibeto-Burman languages

Tibeto-Burman languages are spoken from the Tibetan Plateau in the north to the Malay Peninsula in the south, and from northern Pakistan in the west to northeast Vietnam in the east. Tibeto-Burman languages are, in typology, generally postpositional, SOV languages except for the Karennic and Bai SVO languages. Morphemes are historically monosyllabic.[13] The morphology is generally agglutinative (especially in western Tibeto-Burman languages) with productive compounding processes leading to derivational morphology. Case marking can be ergative, aspectually split-ergative, or nominative-accusative, especially in Tibetan and Kuki-Chin. Diachronic syllable reduction often produces derivational affixes.

Historically, Tibeto-Burman phonology has undergone simplification or dropping of final consonants, reduction of prefixes, and devoicing of initials with the compensatory development of tone (tonogenesis) and increase in vowel distinctions in order to maintain distinctive contrasts. Tone operates at the syllable level. The majority of Tibeto-Burman languages have phonemic tone and/or voice quality contrast, two phonological traits that apparently developed independently.

1.5 Methodology and analysis

Data for this study were obtained from three Zaiwa speakers originally from the Kengtung area of Myanmar and a fourth Zaiwa speaker originally from Yunnan, China, in the time period between October 1993 and March 1995. My two primary Zaiwa co-workers were a female, age 30, and a male, age 22, both from the same village near Kengtung. Texts, sentences, and a wordlist were elicited and utilized in the analysis. All words were recorded in isolation and in a tone frame. Texts acquired were glossed using the Shoebox program. The CECIL (Computerized Extraction of Components of Intonation in Language) program was used to instrumentally verify pitch trajectories. The Findphone program, version 5.7, was used to aid in phonological analysis and to develop a database of sound patterns.

---

[13]A typical Tibeto-Burman morpheme is one syllable long, but compounding is common and words, especially nouns, of two and three syllables often occur.

Introduction

1.6 Overview of the primary research problems and organization of this study

In the Zaiwa language, tone in checked syllables is predictable from voice quality and initial consonant features while tone in unchecked syllables is lexically assigned. Take, for example, the series of words shown in (8). Tone is not marked in the underlying form (UF) since it can be derived at the surface level (SF) from other underlying features.

(8)

Initial consonant/ voice quality	Represents class	UF	SF	
p^h	[−son], voiceless, aspirated	/p^hug/	[p^hɨk^{54}]	'trap fish'
b	[−son], modal voice	/bug/	[bɨk^{32}]	'shoot'
b̰, tense voice	[−son], tense voice	/b̰ug/	[p̰ɨk^{54}]	'kick'
n	[+son], modal voice	/nig/	[nɪk^{32}]	'bamboo'
ṉ, tense voice	[+son], tense voice	/ṉig/	[ṉɪk^{5}]	'heart'

The primary theoretical focus of this study is to present an analysis and representation of tone and voice quality which allows for independent (lexical) tone and also surface level tone dependent on voice quality and initial consonant features (derived tone). It will be shown that the features of [+/−spread vf], [+/−stiff vf] and [+/−const vf] are responsible for the determination of tone at the surface level in checked syllables.

As background to the discussion of segmental and suprasegmental phonology in Zaiwa, chapter 2 discusses the linguistic literature pertaining to Zaiwa phonology including the syllable, consonant inventory and processes, vowel inventory and processes, distribution, tone, and voice quality.

In chapter 3, a phonological review of relevant areas of autosegmental and suprasegmental phonology, feature geometry, pitch and voice quality production, and pitch, voice quality, and segmental feature interaction is presented. This chapter provides the theoretical overview necessary to build the autosegmental framework for the analysis and representation of tone and voice quality in Zaiwa as presented in chapter 4.

In chapter 4, feature geometry is used in combination with underspecification theory to present a framework for describing derived tone based on features of the laryngeal node. A series of rules for the derivation of tone in checked syllables is demonstrated.

This study also describes many other aspects of Zaiwa segmental and suprasegmental phonology in an autosegmental framework and contributes much to demonstrate the applicability of autosegmental phonology to Tibeto-Burman languages.

In chapter 5, aspects of Zaiwa segmental phonology relevant to prosodic studies are considered. The typical syllable is presented as having a bimoraic rhyme, with reduced syllables of various historical origins consisting of a monomoraic rhyme. Of particular interest is the fact that the Zaiwa complex onset may interact with the rhyme to increase syllable weight. The interpretation of the unaspirated, voiceless plosive series as allophones of the voiced plosive series is also discussed. Additional aspects of Zaiwa segmental phonology are found in appendix A.

In chapter 6, additional phonological processes associated with Zaiwa tone and voice quality are discussed. Tone in Zaiwa checked syllables is discussed as a single-tone versus a two-tone interpretation. The evidence presented leads to a single-tone interpretation of pitch in Zaiwa checked syllables. The complexity and options for assignment of voice quality and tone in phonological systems which show interactions between suprasegmental features is also discussed.

2
Previous Studies of Zaiwa Phonology

In this chapter, three previous phonological analyses of Zaiwa will be summarized and examined. These all provide basic descriptions of segments, tone, and voice quality in three different styles or traditions. The first account is that of Burling (1967:16–19), who provides a short description of Zaiwa phonology as a preliminary for a historical reconstruction of Proto-Yi-Burmese. Yabu (1988:105–9) has written a short introduction to Zaiwa phonology as part of a sketch of the Zaiwa language. Xu and Xu (1984:6–20) offer the most complete treatment of Zaiwa phonological features to date. Dai Qingxia (1986) and Dai Qingxia and Yan Mu Chu (1990) have also published short descriptions of Zaiwa phonology. Only the most complete phonological analysis of the three Chinese articles, that of Xu and Xu (1984), will be considered here.

In the following review, Zaiwa phonology will be divided into the major components addressed by the three aforementioned studies: syllable structure, consonant and consonant cluster inventory, phonological processes affecting consonants, vowel inventory, phonological processes affecting vowels, consonant and vowel distribution, tone, and voice quality. The commonalities between the three analyses will be presented in each section first, followed by a discussion of any contrasts in each area. I will include my interpretation of selected phonological features where helpful or where there are major differences from the previous analyses.

2.1 Syllable structure

Syllable structure is discussed by Yabu and Xu and Xu with different interpretations of consonant clusters, and the glottal stop as an initial consonant. Yabu gives the following syllable structure: "an initial consonant (plus a medial consonant) plus a vowel (plus a vowel) (plus a final consonant) plus a tone: C(C)V(V)#/T or C(C)VC/T" (1988:109). In his account there are optional consonant clusters and an obligatory initial consonant (i.e., glottal stop if no other C_i is present). He also makes it clear that a syllable may have either a VV or VC rhyme, but not a VVC. Xu and Xu's analysis of syllables suggests that the pattern is (C)V(V)(C)/T. In their account there are no initial consonant clusters, and a vowel can occur syllable initially (i.e., glottal stop is not interpreted as an initial consonant). Xu and Xu also comment that nasals can form a syllable by themselves, e.g., ɲtaŋ 'ghost tree'.

All three treatments note that there are weak or reduced syllables, and that a vowel in certain non-final syllables can be weakened or reduced to a [ə]. The analyses differ in their interpretation of tone and syllable structure in weak syllables as is shown in the table in (9).

(9) Characteristics of weak syllables in the literature

Characteristic	Burling	Yabu	Xu and Xu
syllable position	nonfinal	initial	first syl of 2-syl word, word internal, not word final
syllable structure		open	open or glottal final
vowel structure	'schwa-like'	weakened	[i] after alveopalatal C_i, [ə] elsewhere
tone contrast	none	low or high	
other	weakly stressed	short vowel	

The most substantive difference between analyses is the differing status of tone contrast in weakened syllables proposed by Burling (no contrast) and Yabu (two tones). In this study, I take the position that there is no contrastive tone in reduced syllables.

2.2 Consonant and consonant cluster inventory

All of the analyses posit the consonant inventory shown in (10) with the points of articulation being labial, alveolar, alveopalatal, palatal, velar, and glottal.[14]

(10) Consonant phonemes included in all analyses

stop vl asp	pʰ	tʰ		kʰ	
stop vl unasp	p	t		k	ʔ
aff vl asp		tsʰ	tʃʰ		
aff vl unasp		ts	tʃ		
fricative		s	ʃ		h
nasal	m	n		ŋ	
lateral		l			
approximant	w	ɹ		j	

Each analysis differs in aspects of distribution, interpretation, and scope. Burling's unaspirated stop series is voiced. He also adds glottalized series of obstruents, nasals, and a liquid, /pʔ tʔ kʔ mʔ nʔ ŋʔ lʔ/, which contrast with the plain and aspirated series. In this study I posit both a voiceless aspirated and voiced series of stops underlyingly, and treat voice quality as a suprasegmental feature rather than part of a consonant series.

The phonemes /w ɹ h/ are assigned differing phonemic values in the three articles as shown in (11).

(11) Differing interpretations of /w ɹ h/

Phoneme	Burling	Yabu	Xu and Xu
/w/	/v/, vd labial fricative	/w/	/v/
/ɹ/	/r/, retroflex, fricative	/r/	/ʒ/
/h/	/h/, some friction	/x/	/x/

Xu and Xu use /ʒ/ instead of /ɹ/, which would set up a pattern of congruity with /ʃ/. Other choices seem to be based on phonetic similarity and choice from different allophonic variants (see §2.3). Xu and Xu also include the phoneme /f/ in their inventory, noting that it only occurs in

---

[14]Burling's phonemic chart does not include /ʔ/ or /j/. This is likely an oversight since both these segments appear in his transcriptions. The manners of articulation and points of articulation used in (10) are the best estimation of those which fit the phonemic inventories of each analysis.

borrowed words from Han Chinese. In this study I interpret the phonemes in (11) as /w ɹ h/.

A major difference among the three phonemes concerns the issue of consonant clusters versus unitary initials with secondary articulations. Xu and Xu assume Zaiwa has no consonant clusters. Consonant/palatal glide combinations are considered to be single phonological segments. This adds /pʰʲ pʰ mʲ kʰʲ kʲ ŋʲ xʲ/ to Xu and Xu's phonemic inventory. Burling and Yabu both treat /pʰʲ pʲ mʲ kʰʲ kʲ/ as consonant clusters. Burling also includes /nj/. Yabu uses /ñ/ as a single segment instead of a consonant cluster in his phonemic inventory. Xu and Xu interpret [nj] as the result of an allophonic process as discussed in §2.3. Neither Burling nor Yabu analyze /ŋj xʲ/ as clusters in the manner of Xu and Xu's palatalized segments. Yabu also includes /kr/ as a consonant cluster. In this study I interpret the consonant/glide combinations as consonant clusters, including /nj/.

2.3 Phonological processes affecting consonants

All analysts agree that final stops are unreleased. All other accounts of phonological processes affecting consonants vary considerably.

Burling's /v/ has bilabial friction preceding /e/ and /a/ in high tone syllables and rather wide free variation, approaching a [w] in other positions. Yabu assumes that the phoneme /w/ becomes a weak fricative [v] preceding /o u/ and becomes [w] preceding other vowels.

In Yabu's analysis, the underlying forms /p t k c ts/ are realized as voiceless [p t k c ts] when they precede glottalized (creaky) vowels. The same series becomes [b̥ d̥ g̊ d̥ʒ d̥z̥] (on-glide devoiced, off-glide half-voiced) preceding nonglottalized vowels. Xu and Xu call all stops and affricates voiceless and do not comment on voicing changes in tense versus lax syllables. In this study I present the voiced plosive series as devoicing in tense syllables. Yabu also states that /x/ varies freely between [x] and [h] when preceding /i/.

According to Xu and Xu, alveolar consonants are palatalized when followed by /i/, /e/, or their tense voice counterparts, e.g., /thi/→ [thji] 'grapes for wine'.

2.4 Vowel inventory

All analyses agree that the Zaiwa simple vowels are /i e a o u/ and that the diphthongs include /au ai ui/. Yabu and Xu and Xu also recognize a diphthong /oi/. Both Yabu and Xu and Xu include a creaky or tense series of vowels in parallel to the lax series. Burling comments that

/ui/ sounds almost bisyllabic and occurs with only one tone. He considers /ui/ to be a diphthong instead of a /wi/ series due to the absence of any other vowels following a medial /w/.

2.5 Phonological processes affecting vowels

Burling (1967:18) states "All vowels except /a/ are lowered somewhat in stopped syllables as compared with unstopped syllables."

Xu and Xu state that /e/ and /e̱/[15] become [ə] following bilabials, alveolars, velars, and /v/. When /e/ occurs alone, it is realized as [ə], whereas when /e̱/ occurs alone, it is realized as [e]. /i/ and /i̱/ become [ɤ][16] following velars, or following bilabials, alveolars, and /v/ while preceding /k ŋ ʔ/.

2.6 Consonant and vowel distribution

Burling as well as Xu and Xu include all consonants except glottal stop as initials while Yabu also includes the glottal stop. All analyses agree that initial consonants in glottalized syllables include /p t k ts tsʃ m n ŋ l/. Yabu and Xu and Xu also include /w j/. In addition Yabu adds /ñ ʃ x ʔ/ and Xu and Xu add /ʒ/.

All analyses propose /p t k ʔ m n ŋ/ as finals.

Yabu reports the distribution of all VC combinations with both non-glottalized and glottalized vowels in nonborrowed Zaiwa words, except for */ep et ek em en eŋ ip im uk/. Xu and Xu give only */im ip/ as exceptions. Burling and Yabu note that diphthongs are not followed by syllable-final stops or nasals.

2.7 Tone

Each analysis assumes Zaiwa has at least three tones: I, a low-level or low-falling tone; II, a high-level tone; and III, a high-falling tone. Yabu and Xu and Xu both present basically the same analysis of tone as shown in (12).[17]

---

[15]Xu and Xu underline a vowel to transcribe tense voice.

[16][ɤ] is a mid back unrounded vocoid.

[17]Yabu uses a 4–1 scale, and Xu and Xu use a 5–1 scale. I have given Yabu's 4 the value of 5 for this chart. Yabu divides tone 1 into two allotonic variants based on syllable type: (1) low-level, long [22] in open or nasal-final syllables; (2) low-level or low-falling, short [22 ~ 21] in stopped syllables.

(12)   Yabu and Xu and Xu's tone systems

    Tone I   21
    Tone II   55
    Tone III   51

Yabu and Xu and Xu allow only tones I and II in checked syllables and all tones in unchecked syllables. Burling's tone system is more complex and includes variation based on grammatical parts of speech and only a single stopped tone. Burling posits five tones summarized as follows:[18]

1 Low, falling, and moderately long. This tone does not occur on verbs.
2 Falling, but short and not as low as 1. Only occurs with verbs. Followed by certain suffixes, tone 2 is a mid, even, long tone. Followed by other suffixes, tone 2 is a short, falling tone. Tone 2 could be combined with tone 1 since it does not occur with nonverbs, but this simplification went against the intuition of Burling's informant.
3 High, short, and falling.
4 High, more even, and longer than any of the other tones.
5 Stopped tone. All stopped syllables are considered to have a single tone with different phonetic manifestation depending on initial consonant and voice quality (see §6.4 for further explanation).

A summary of the tone interpretations is shown in (13). Burling's tones 1 and 2 correspond to Tone I, Burling's tone 4 corresponds with Tone II, and Burling's tone 3 corresponds with Tone III. Burling's stopped tone allotones correlate with the lexical tones assigned to stopped syllables by Yabu and Xu and Xu.

(13)

	Xu and Xu, Yabu	Burling
Tone I	21 (checked and unchecked syllables)	low, falling (not on verbs)
		low, falling, short, (only on verbs)
Tone II	55 (checked and unchecked syllables)	high, even, long
Tone III	51	high, short, falling
Checked tone	allotones of tone I and II	variants of a unique tone

---

[18]The tones are numbered here for convenience and do not correspond to any tone numbering presented by Burling.

Previous Studies of Zaiwa Phonology

In this study I posit three lexical tones (53, 4, 31), and a single derived tone in checked syllables with tone height depending on features of the initial consonant and voice quality. Discussion of the historical development of Zaiwa tonal categories is outside the scope of this study. Burling (1967) gives an account of the place of Zaiwa tones in Proto-Lolo-Burmese.

Xu and Xu give the following explanations of tonal variations:
1. [55] becomes [15] when the syllable begins with an unaspirated consonant (excluding voiceless fricatives) and the vowel is lax.
2. The three tones in weak syllables are 'soft' and are pronounced 'soft' and short.[19] [55] and [51] become a [55] 'soft' tone. [21] becomes a [21] 'soft' tone.
3. Tone changes are presented as complex and related to the types of words formed and the type of sentence the words occur in. In the five examples in (14) [31] becomes [51], [51] becomes [31], and [55] becomes [51] when the syllables are unchecked in the indicated environments. [31] becomes [55] and [55] becomes [31] when the syllables are checked in the indicated environments.

(14)   noun ('soft' tone) + pe^{55} (plural suffix)
'rapid' tone occurring following the 'soft' tone
verb or adj. ('soft' tone) + e^{55} (adjectivized particle)
verb or adj. ('soft' tone) + za^{55} (affirmative particle)
verb or adj. ('soft' tone) in indicative or interrogative sentences.

2.8 Voice quality

The three analyses differ on their interpretation of voice quality distinctions.

Burling (1967:16) assumes a creaky-clear contrast in voice quality for which glottalized versus nonglottalized initial consonants are responsible. Creaky vowels are produced by "a constriction of the muscles of the larynx." He comments further that "In all likelihood this 'creaky' voice quality is initiated by a release of the stopped glottis occurring simultaneously or very shortly after the release of the other articulators, although no marked glottal stop is audible" (pp. 16–17).

Yabu (1988:107) assumes glottalization to be an aspect of the vowel, distinguishing a glottalized (creaky) and a nonglottalized vowel system. He characterizes a glottalized vowel as being "pronounced with an extreme tension in the larynx in the duration of the vowel sound." Nasals preceding glottalized vowels are pronounced as preglottalized nasals.

---

[19]'Soft' tones correspond to tones in unchecked syllables and 'rapid' tones correspond to tones in checked syllables.

Xu and Xu place tense and lax distinctions on the vowels, similar to Yabu.

In this study I propose that tense voice quality is assigned to the initial consonant as an autosegment, and spreads to the following vowel, giving the characteristic tense vowel quality.

2.9 Discussion

Some of the more obvious areas of difference among the writers are the proposed characteristics of weak syllables, the status of /j h v r ?/, the occurrence of voiced stops and affricates, the palatalization of alveolar consonants, the number and distribution of tones, and the status of marked versus modal voice quality. In particular, Burling contends that weak syllables are toneless while Yabu posits two contrastive tones. Burling and Yabu analyzed consonant/glide combinations as clusters while Xu and Xu analyze them as single units. Burling includes a voiced series of stops, Yabu splits this into partially-voiced and voiceless allophones, and Xu and Xu call the series voiceless. Burling adds a glottalized series of consonants to account for marked voice quality while the others attribute voice quality differences to the vowels. There is also considerable difference in which phonological processes are treated. Some analyses cover everything included in the other analyses. All analyses leave out large portions of phonological processes and discussion of phonological motivation for the processes that are included. The analyses do, however, provide a good starting point for further study of the Zaiwa phonological system.

3
Phonological Prerequisites to the Analysis and Representation of Zaiwa Phonology

In order to develop a framework for the analysis and representation of Zaiwa phonology, certain phonological concepts and prior phonological research related to the salient aspects of Zaiwa phonology must be reviewed. This chapter will introduce the necessary phonological prerequisites to the development of a framework for the analysis and representation of segmental and suprasegmental aspects of Zaiwa phonology. First, analytical and representational aspects of autosegmental phonology (§3.1), feature geometry (§3.2), and underspecification theory (§3.3) will be reviewed in order to introduce the phonological theories upon which the analysis will draw. A review of pitch and voice quality, their mechanisms, and their interaction with each other and with segments (§3.4) will supply the necessary background for understanding the phonological processes which necessitate the phonological framework for analysis and representation presented in chapter 4.

3.1 Overview of autosegmental phonology assumptions

In autosegmental phonology, speech is cut vertically into segments and horizontally into sequences of features. Each sequence of features is isolated on a tier. The tiers are associated using association lines which connect autosegments on one tier to the appropriate autosegments on another tier. These association lines represent "simultaneity in time" of production of the features (Goldsmith 1990:10). A central or skeletal tier can be utilized as a point of attachment for all features of autosegmental tiers which associate to a single position in the syllable structure, including the segmental tier (15). The skeletal tier is represented by Xs or C and V slots.

(15) 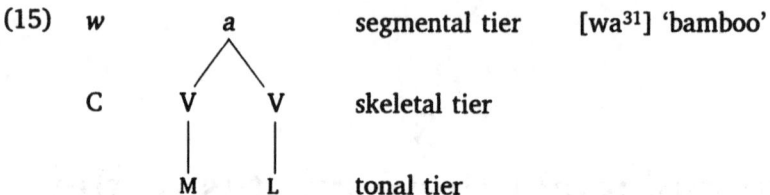 [wa^{31}] 'bamboo'

Goldsmith (1990) gives the formal representations for autosegmental phonology in (16).

(16) 1. Unbroken association lines represent existing associations.
2. A broken association line represents a structural change.

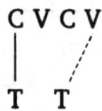

3. A circle around a segment in a rule marks a segment unassociated with an autosegment on the facing tier.

4. An 'x' on an association line indicates that the line is to be deleted.

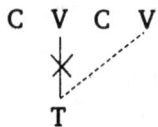

Autosegmental phonology allows a many-to-one mapping of features to slots on the skeletal tier and a graphic representation of phonological processes. Spreading (17) and deletion (18) are both common processes.

Phonological Prerequisites

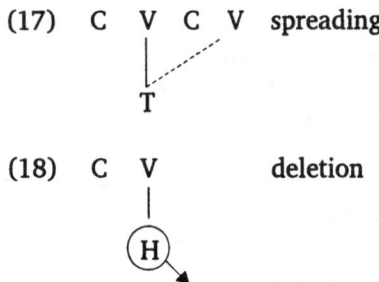

(17)   C   V   C   V   spreading

(18)   C   V   deletion

Following Goldsmith's model, tone is represented autosegmentally on a tonal tier and is mapped to tone bearing units (TBUs) on the segmental or skeletal tier and may spread freely across segments. The associations are subject to the well-formedness condition of Goldsmith (1976:27) as shown in (19).

(19)   Well-formedness condition (WFC)

   a. All vowels are associated with at least one tone.
   b. Every tone is associated with at least one vowel.
   c. Association lines do not cross.

The direction of mapping tones to TBUs follows the universal association convention (Pulleyblank 1983:31) as shown in (20).

(20)   Map a sequence of tones onto a sequence of tone bearing units,

   a. from left to right
   b. in a one-to-one relation.

The aspects of autosegmental phonology discussed in this section will be applied to the analysis and representation of Zaiwa phonology.

3.2 Overview of phonological features and feature geometry

Phonological segments can be broken down into simultaneously occurring phonological features. The application of features to segments has traditionally been seen as groupings of features occurring at the same time with no internal organization. The matrix of phonological features and segments which characterized phonological analysis were gradually supplanted in the late 1970s and early 1980s as autosegmental phonology gained acceptance. In the early 1980s, linguists observed that certain sets of features behave as a unit with respect to phonological rules of assimilation and deletion. Clements (1985) captured these generalizations in feature geometry in which distinctive features have internal structure. Autosegmental tiers are not all linked to the skeletal tier directly, but instead there is a hierarchical arrangement of class nodes on separate tiers between the actual autosegmental features and the skeletal tier. The top node is the root node which includes [+/−son] and [+/−cons] and associates directly to the skeletal tier. Nonterminal nodes designate articulators, and terminal nodes designate distinctive features. Adaptations to the Clements (1985) model have stricture features directly dominated by the root node and associated with a particular articulator by convention. Feature geometry is useful in showing the relationships between distinctive features. Features are organized into trees defined by the organization of nodes and associations between the nodes. Assimilation processes can spread a node from the feature tree of one segment to another provided that there is no identical node between the nodes involved.

A common organization used in feature geometry is that of Halle (1992) as shown in (21).

(21) Feature geometry organization

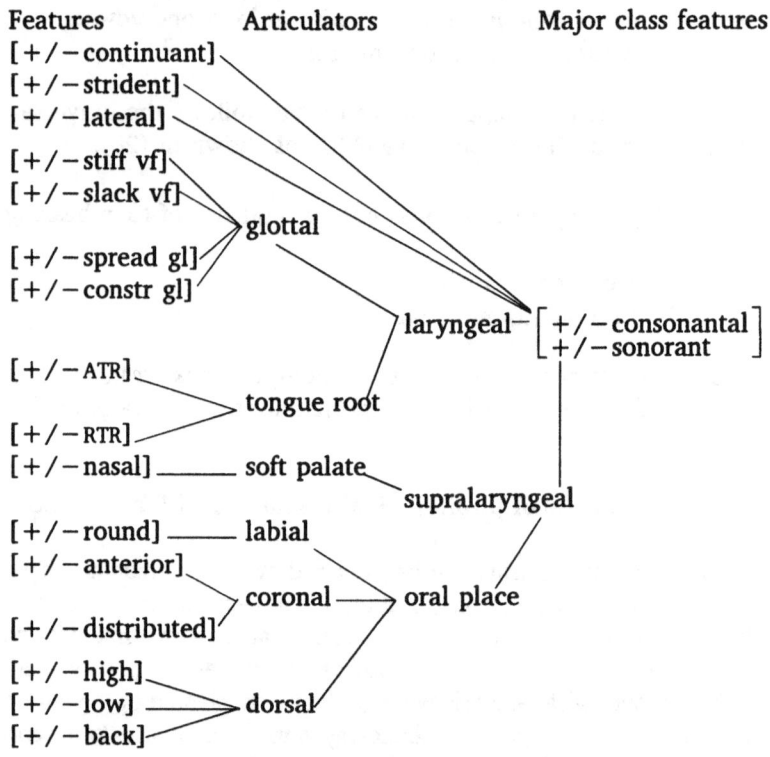

Adjustments to this model will be made as necessary for Zaiwa phonology (see §4.4.1).

3.3 Overview of underspecification theory

Underspecification is a form of feature representation which allows only non-redundant features and marked features to appear in the underlying form of a phonological unit. Pulleyblank states that underspecification requires that:

> all redundancy be eliminated from underlying representations. In particular, only non-redundant feature values may be included in underlying representations; predictable feature values are filled by redundancy rules—rules that are of a highly constrained nature. A central claim of this theory is that most redundancy rules are not language-specific rules; they are either (a) provided by Universal Grammar (default rules) or (b) derived by a general principle of Universal Grammar (Complement Rules). (1986:123)

Default rules are generally context-free and apply to every distinctive feature. The default feature for a unit does not occur in the underlying representation. Default rules fill in the unmarked case. An example of a default rule is "all [+son] segments are [+voice]" ([+son]→ [+voice]). There is a standard rule ordering for the application of default rules.[20] For this study it is sufficient to say that default rules apply after all other phonological rules have applied.

3.4 Overview of pitch and voice quality production and interactions

Contrastive pitch and tense versus modal voice quality are the two most salient suprasegmentals in Zaiwa. The production and variations of both are determined by the features and settings of the larynx. In §3.4.1, the anatomy and physiology of the larynx will be reviewed as a background for understanding tone and voice quality distinctions. In §3.4.2, pitch production will be reviewed. In §3.4.3, relevant aspects of the interaction of pitch with segments will be reviewed. In §3.4.4, voice quality production will be discussed. Finally, in §3.4.5, aspects of the interaction of pitch with voice quality will be discussed as they relate to processes which occur in Zaiwa phonology.

---

[20]See Pulleyblank (1986) for more details.

3.4.1 The anatomy and physiology of the larynx

In order to understand the production of pitch and contrastive voice qualities in Zaiwa and their interaction with each other and with segments, a brief discussion of the anatomy and physiology of the larynx, with an emphasis on phonatory settings[21] and tension settings as presented in Laver (1980), will serve as background. The larynx is made of three types of cartilages, the vocal folds, and the connecting muscles. The THYROID CARTILAGE, the CRICOID CARTILAGE, and the two ARYTENOID CARTILAGES are the points of attachment for the vocal folds and are also the fixed structures that other muscles position in the processes of forming phonatory settings. The figure in (22) shows a left side view of the major components of the larynx.

(22)

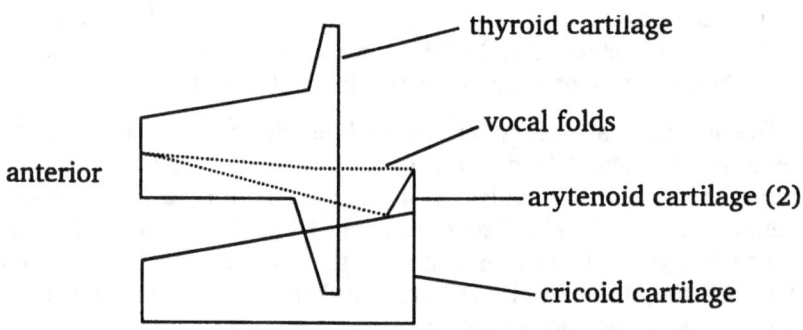

Each cartilage is connected to the vocal folds by various muscles. Three types of muscular tension, produced by the interaction of the cartilages, muscles, and vocal folds, define different laryngeal settings which affect voice quality and pitch. These muscular parameters are ADDUCTIVE TENSION, MEDIAL COMPRESSION, and LONGITUDINAL TENSION. Adductive tension can bring the vocal folds together to allow voicing or completely close the glottis as in a glottal stop. Medial compression is defined by Laver (1980:108) as "the compressional pressure on the vocal processes of the arytenoid cartilages achieved by contraction of the lateral cricoarytenoid muscles and reinforced by tension in the lateral parts of the thyroarytenoid muscles." Medial tension will close the ligamental glottis. Medial compression, therefore, also contributes to the closing of

---

[21]Phonatory settings are the settings of the members of the larynx in order to produce a specific phonation type. Laver (1994:184) defines phonation as "the use of the laryngeal system, with the help of an airstream provided by the respiratory system, to generate an audible source of acoustic energy which can then be modified by the articulatory actions of the rest of the vocal apparatus."

the vocal folds. Longitudinal tension is basically the contraction of the vocal folds themselves, making them tense. The geometric relationship between the three parameters is shown from a top view in the figure in (23), which is adapted from Laver (p. 109).

(23)

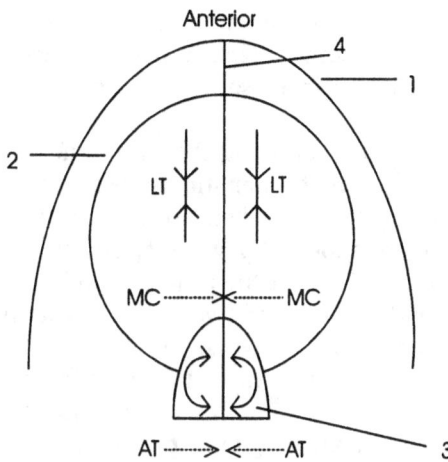

LT	- longitudinal tension	1. thyroid cartilage
MC	- medial compression	2. cricoid cartilage
AT	- adductive tension	3. arytenoid cartilages
		4. ligamental glottis

The vocal folds vibrate as air flows across them when they are brought together by adductive tension and/or medial compression. The amount of airflow depends on the size of the glottal aperture and the tension on the vocal folds. The rate of vibration depends on vocal fold tension and subglottal pressure.[22] With this basic understanding of the larynx, the production and interactions of pitch and voice qualities can now be discussed.

3.4.2 Pitch production

Pitch variation that affects the meaning of words, i.e., that is contrastive, is the major (but not the only) concomitant of phonological tone and is a part of the Zaiwa phonological system. Pitch is produced when air from the lungs passes through the vocal folds, making them vibrate regularly. The pitch produced is dependent upon three variables, each of

---

[22]Subglottal pressure is defined as "the air-pressure in the pulmonic airstream just below the vocal folds" (Laver 1994:163).

which are relevant to the interaction of pitch, voicing, and voice quality in Zaiwa:
1. The tension on the vocal folds is the primary determinant of pitch. Stretching the vocal folds in the anterior-posterior direction raises pitch. An increase in vocal fold tension raises pitch while a decrease lowers pitch. Raising the larynx also increases tension on the vocal folds and raises pitch while lowering the larynx lowers pitch.
2. Pulmonic air flow or the air pressure difference above and below the glottis (subglottal pressure) affects pitch. An increase in subglottal pressure raises pitch. An increase in the rate of air flow through the glottis raises pitch.
3. The position of the vocal folds and the width and length of the glottal aperture produce different phonation types and pitch capabilities. Pitch is normally manifested when voicing occurs, therefore, glottal closure must be close enough for voicing, but not so close that vibration is stopped or so wide that the airflow is unimpeded. The range of glottal aperture within which stiff vocal folds will vibrate is narrower than that for slack vocal folds, and the subglottal pressure must be increased for voicing to occur with stiff vocal folds.

The production of pitch is a complex interaction between vocal fold tension, glottal aperture size, subglottal pressure, and airflow. Although each of these parameters can be controlled independently, they can also affect each other. Each of these factors can be varied actively or unintentionally through another speech process. The activity of the laryngeal muscles on the vocal folds is the primary mechanism by which pitch changes are actively produced. Actively controlling pitch by changing subglottal pressure is questioned by Ohala (1973:6) who says, "The extent to which pitch is actively regulated by variations of the expiratory force is negligible."

3.4.3 The interaction of pitch with segments

The presence of phonological segments at certain positions in the syllable and the features of phonological segments can affect tone. Phonological segments, such as syllable onsets and codas, help to define the domain of tone. Phonological features of segments, such as voicing, sonority, and glottal constriction can affect tone production.

Haudricourt (1954) was one of the first to present an analysis of the correlations between final consonant types and tone in Asian languages. The effect of initials was originally discussed by Edkins (1853) and Steinthal (1855) and later by Maspero (1912). Since that time, many Tibeto-Burmanists have studied the interaction between tone and the phonological features of consonants. Consonant types in Tibeto-Burman languages affect tone height and contour. The production of contrastive pitch due to the loss of consonant voicing and final consonants is one of the key factors in tonogenesis in Tibeto-Burman languages. Matisoff (1973b:21) states that "The development of tones in the Lolo-Burmese languages has been influenced primarily by the manner of articulation of the syllable-initial consonant." Initial voiced consonants in the proto-language correlate with lower tones, and voiceless or aspirated consonants correlate with higher tones. Initial consonant voicing only affects the register[23] of the following tone, not the contour (p. 76). There is some evidence that aspirated stops raise tone more than voiceless unaspirated stops, which raise tone more than voiced stops (Mazaudon 1976:6). Bradley (1982:1) distinguishes initial consonants and final consonants by their effect on tone with "initial consonants conditioning pitch height, and certain 'laryngeal' final consonants often conditioning the development of pitch contour." A final glottal stop tends to cause a rising pitch contour and a final [h] tends to cause a falling contour (Bradley 1977:2, Matisoff 1973b:75).[24] Glover (1971:13) discusses the interaction of initial and final consonants with register for Tibeto-Burman languages in the Gurung branch; "The initial symbol dominates the final in determining the register of the word but the final determines (usually) secondary features."

These tendencies are exploited differently by different languages. Some languages, such as Rawang, currently show no correlation between consonant voicing and tones (Morse 1962:69). Other languages, such as some dialects of Jinghpaw, show complete redundancy between consonant voicing and tones (Maran 1971). Still others, such as Zaiwa, are at an intermediate stage with correlation between consonant voicing and tone in checked syllables, but not in unchecked syllables. This review of the complete range of the correlation between tone and consonant voicing shows that, within the same language family, features can range from having independent control to complete dependency.

One explanation for the effect of initial consonant voicing on tone is based on differences in subglottal pressure and airflow associated with different glottal apertures. Airflow through a constriction in a tube causes

---

[23]The term register has two different uses in Tibeto-Burman languages. Register can refer to tone space, dividing the pitch range in two, or register can be used of a bundling of features including phonation types such as creaky or breathy voice as it is commonly used in the discussion of Mon-Khmer languages. A third reference to register occurs in register versus contour systems (Pike 1948), where a register tone system only contains tones of different discrete heights, and a contour tone system may have rising and falling tones as well as level pitch tones.

[24]Phonetic motivation for these processes is as follows: a glottal stop decreases the glottal aperture and increases vocal fold tension, resulting in a rise in pitch. An [h] does just the opposite resulting in a lowering of pitch. See later discussion in this section for further differentiation of contour tone in relation to variations of glottal stop.

a vacuum at the point where air enters the tube. The higher the airflow, the greater the vacuum pressure. This is called the BERNOULLI EFFECT. The Bernoulli effect produces a negative pressure on air in the lungs as air passes through the larynx. A spread glottis allows less impeded and swifter airflow and hence an increase in the Bernoulli effect. The increase and decrease in pitch related to voicing is caused by variations of pressure caused by the Bernoulli effect. A syllable-initial voiceless or aspirated segment with modal voice has a spread glottis and induces a large Bernoulli effect. The high rate of airflow vibrates the vocal folds at a higher frequency as they come together for voicing on the following glide or vowel. Ohala states that,

> Upon release of a voiceless aspirated consonant . . . the rate of air flow is initially very high, since there is momentarily little resistance to the air flow at the open glottis or in the oral cavity. Thus when the vocal cords do adduct for voicing they meet a very high rate of air flow and consequently vibrate at an initially high rate, gradually returning to their "normal" rate of vibration. (1973:8)

A voiced initial, however, decreases airflow through the glottis due to the greater glottal constriction necessary for voicing and does not allow a large Bernoulli effect. The rate of vibration of the vocal folds during the production of the following vowel is not markedly increased, and lower pitch results (Ladefoged 1973).

Syllable-final consonants can also affect tone. The presence of syllable-final voiceless stops tends to limit the number of tones in checked syllables (Benedict 1948:184). Some Tibeto-Burman languages, such as Rawang (Morse 1962:69) and Burmese (Burling 1966:584), show only a single tone in checked syllables. Other languages, such as the Shanghai dialect of Chinese (Benedict 1948:185) and Zaiwa, have only a single tone in checked syllables, but the tone is allotonically influenced by the voicing of the initial consonant. Still other languages, such as Lahu (Matisoff 1973a:23) and Maru (Burling 1967:21), have two contrastive tones in checked syllables due to a historical tonal split and final stop epenthesis,[25] respectively.

In Tibeto-Burman languages, syllable-final /p t k/ are actually co-articulated [pʔ tʔ kʔ]. Diehl (1992b:6) states this explicitly; "anyone who has done much language study in East and Southeast Asia knows that a syllable-final glottal stop is often an abandoned companion to a former (co-articulated) oral stop." The final stops are all present in some

---

[25]Burling (1966) notes that Maru has two types of checked syllables. Those which correspond to Zaiwa checked syllables and follow the same tonal variations depending on initial consonant voicing, and those which have an "intrusive" final stop which do not show correspondence in tone and initial consonant voicing.

languages (Zaiwa, Maru, Lashi, Rawang), but in others (Phunoi, Bisu, Northern Burmese) some of the stops have reduced to a /ʔ/, and in still others (Lahu, Akha, Standard Burmese), all final stops have reduced to a /ʔ/. Further reduction is recorded in still other Tibeto-Burman languages where the /ʔ/ has disappeared with the only remnant being laryngealization (Hani, Yi). This process of reduction, or debuccalization, does away with the oral stop portion of the segment but tends to leave the glottal stop intact.

This co-articulation makes it reasonable to assume that oral stop finals could have a similar effect on tone as the final glottal stops. In some cases this is true, and in others the affect differs. Both oral and glottal stop codas contribute to a rise in tone height in languages such as Zaiwa when the initial is a [+spread vf] obstruent. The glottal constriction contributed by the glottal stop coda is the primary factor here. Tone in checked, nontense syllables with [+spread vf] initials is raised due to the Bernoulli effect on the vowel. The syllable starts out with a [+spread vf] consonant and ends with a glottalized ([+const vf]) consonant, and the vowel or glide-vowel combination is in between. The glottis goes from fully open to closed as the shortened vowel is pronounced, which raises pitch. Greater respiratory force may also be used. Maddieson and Ladefoged (1985:441) show a correlation between syllables closed with a glottal stop and greater respiratory force when compared with open syllables in Jinghpaw. The increase in respiratory force, manifested as increased subglottal pressure, could vibrate the vocal cords faster and raise pitch. This may contribute to the rise in pitch shown in Zaiwa checked syllables.

Co-articulated oral/glottal stops and glottal stops can also have a somewhat different affect on tone. In Zaiwa, a syllable final co-articulated oral/glottal stop allows partial to no tone fall while a glottal stop allows a partial to full tone fall. This will be discussed in general now and expanded specifically in relation to Zaiwa in §6.3.1.

The correlation between glottal stop and a fall in pitch would seem to disagree with the commonly held belief that glottal stop raises pitch resulting in rising contours, as seen in Vietnamese (Haudricourt 1954). The fact is that there are two types of glottal stops, each having a different effect on the preceding tone. Mazaudon (1976:65) states that "the expected effect of final glottal stop is a rising pitch, as in Vietnamese or Archaic Chinese. On the contrary the effect of an imperfect glottal closure appears to be a falling pitch." This parallels the relationship between Burmese creaky tone, which falls near the end of the tone due to 'leakage' of air through the glottis, and Burmese checked tone, which is level with a final glottal stop which checks airflow (Lehman 1991:7, Maran 1971:128). This interpretation gives a four-way distinction in the affect that final consonants have on tone contour. The effects are summarized in (24).

(24)   Final   Effect on tone

1. Sonorant or open syllable   Full tonal realization or fall
2. Oral plosive, or co-articulation   Extreme tone shortening and
   of oral plosive and incomplete   suppression of fall
   glottal closure
3. Incomplete glottal closure   Intermediate tone shortening
                                       and suppression of fall
4. Complete glottal closure   Tone shortening and rise of
                                       contour

Both types of glottal stop can contribute to raising pitch register when in the coda position, as discussed earlier in this section. They both, however, have a differing affect on tone contour.

The transfer of initial consonant and final consonant features to the vocalic nucleus to produce tone is well attested (Matisoff 1973b, Maran 1973). Maran presents more insight into the internal structure of this transfer. He states that "the initial based transfer mechanism does not seem to apply without the final based mechanism", and "the final-based mechanisms apply originally and then the initial-based mechanisms enter the derivation of tones" (p. 111). His "biconditional" process is shown in (25).

(25)   Given C_1VC_2:

i. $V \rightarrow Vx/\_\ C_2$
ii. $V \rightarrow Vy/C_1\ \_$
iii. Thus, $C_1VC_2 \rightarrow C_1VxyC_2$ (as a result of i. and ii.)[26]

The biconditional process is relevant to Zaiwa checked syllables in which the glottal constriction of the final stop and the [+/−spread vf] and [+/−const vf] features of the initial consonant work together to determine tone. It seems that the process in Zaiwa is only relevant when both C_1 and C_2 work simultaneously, as there is no observable individual effects on pitch from C_1 and C_2 independent of each other.

---

[26]Maran (1973:111) interchanged the consonants in his chart giving C_2VC_1. I have changed them to C_1VC_2 for consistency with the rest of the book.

3.4.4 Voice quality production

Laver, in his landmark work *The Phonetic Description of Voice Quality*, defines voice quality as follows:

> Voice quality is conceived here in a broad sense, as the characteristic auditory colouring of an individual speaker's voice, and not in the more narrow sense of the quality deriving solely from laryngeal activity. Both laryngeal and supralaryngeal features will be seen as contributing to voice quality. Perceptually, voice quality in this broad interpretation is a cumulative abstraction over a period of time of a speaker-characterizing quality, which is gathered from the momentary and spasmodic fluctuations of short-term articulations used by the speaker for linguistic and paralinguistic communication. Following Abercrombie, the term "voice quality" will be taken to refer to "those characteristics which are present more or less all the time that a person is talking: it is a quasi-permanent quality running through all the sound that issues from his mouth" (Abercrombie 1967:91). (1980:1)

Voice quality is considered to be an auditory setting which runs over a sequence of segments. "Settings give a background, auditory 'colouring' running through sequences of shorter-term segmental articulations" (p. 2). This interpretation of voice quality lends itself to an autosegmental framework for analysis.

Many (but not all) voice qualities depend on the size of the glottal aperture. Adductive tension and medial compression work to close the glottis resulting in a range of glottal constriction from complete closure, e.g., [+const vf] for a glottal stop, to a completely open glottis, e.g., [+spread vf] for voiceless or aspirated segments. Other voice qualities are somewhere in between.

In addition to, or in combination with aperture settings are tension settings throughout the vocal tract, which also affect voice quality. TENSE VOICE has a high degree of tension throughout the vocal system (including the pharynx) while LAX VOICE has a low degree of tension. The NEUTRAL or MODAL VOICE is midway between tense and lax tension settings. Tense voice has high adductive tension and high medial compression which constrict the glottis. Tense voice also has high longitudinal tension which gives a higher frequency of vibration.

In Zaiwa, aperture and tension settings combine to give voiceless or aspirated, voiced, creaky, tense, and glottal stop laryngeal states. Ladefoged (1972) addresses three of these, giving graphic representations of the voiceless, voiced, and creaky voice states of the glottis. In (26), Ladefoged's representations are borrowed, and tense voice and glottal stop representations are added to complete the range of laryngeal states present in Zaiwa.

(26) anterior larynx

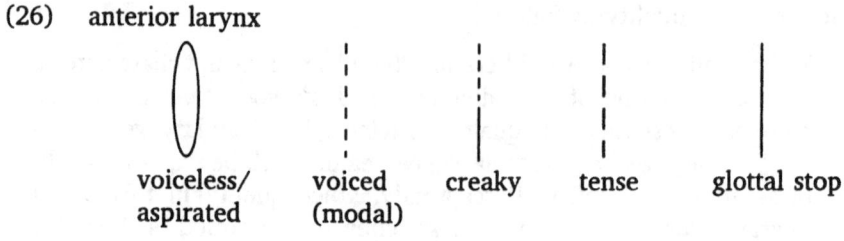

      voiceless/   voiced   creaky   tense   glottal stop
      aspirated   (modal)

posterior larynx

(Vibrating parts of the vocal folds are indicated by normal dashed lines, closed parts of the glottis are indicated by solid lines, and tense and constricted glottis are indicated by the bold dashed line.)

In the voiceless/aspirated glottal state the vocal folds are too far apart to vibrate. Voicing is allowed under normal subglottal pressure when the vocal folds are brought close together, but not tightly closed. In the closed portion of creaky voice, in tense voice, and with the glottal stop, the vocal folds are too close to vibrate at normal subglottal pressure.[27] In creaky voice, vibration is allowed with normal subglottal pressure at the anterior end of the vocal folds, bubbling through the lax vocal folds. Tense vocal folds, although constricted, can vibrate with increased subglottal pressure. In tense voice the vocal folds begin vibration once subglottal pressure is sufficient to vibrate the stiff vocal folds. Sonorants with tense voice quality are voiced because the lack of constriction in the oral cavity allows free airflow with an increase in subglottal pressure which is sufficient to vibrate tense vocal folds. Voicing is not heard on tense voice nonsonorants due to the oral occlusion which does not allow air to pass through the vocal folds at a sufficient rate to vibrate them.[28] Voicing of sonorants which follow nonsonorants, begins just after the release of the articulatory occlusion or stricture.

---

[27]The correlation between phonation and subglottal pressure is demonstrated in two studies which correlate airflow and glottal aperture. In the first study, Maddieson and Ladefoged (1985:436) show that "for any given subglottal pressure the airflow will be greater when the vocal cords are vibrating in the comparatively lax way ... conversely the airflow will be less during a more tense, slightly laryngealized, or creaky voiced vowel." In the second study, Edmondson and Shaoni (1995) measured maximum phonation time for breathy, lax, and tense syllables. They showed that breathy voice had the shortest airflow time which corresponds to the highest airflow, while tense voice had the longest airflow time corresponding to the lowest airflow and, hence, highest subglottal pressure.

The origin of tense voice is relevant to a discussion of tense voice production. Three origins have been suggested for tense voice. The Chinese linguists Hu Tan and Dai Qingxia (1964) first attributed the tense/lax voice distinction in Yi-Burmese languages to a loss of stopped syllable codas. In this model the larynx is tense in anticipation of a final stop. When the stop is gradually lost over time through sound change, the tenseness stays as the displaced contrast on the vowel. Burling (1967) attributes "creaky" voice[29] to a preglottalized series in Proto-Tibeto-Burman. Yang Huandian (1990) claims that, in the case of Naxi,[30] the tense/lax voice distinction is an inherent feature of the proto-language and also a feature of Proto-Tibeto-Burman. All three possibilities could hold true for tense voice formation in Zaiwa, assuming that Hu Tan and Dai Qingxia's model allows some final stops to reduce to a glottal, while others do not, since Zaiwa has not lost its final stops. The processes proposed may all be valid in Tibeto-Burman, producing phonation distinctions in different languages in different ways.[31]

A neutral or "modal" phonatory setting must be defined as a standard by which to discuss or compare a marked setting. The modal setting of the larynx and vocal apparatus, which will contrast with that of tense voice in Zaiwa, is characterized by the following specifications:

> the vibration of the true vocal folds is regularly periodic, efficient in air use, without audible friction, with the folds in full glottal vibration under moderate longitudinal tension, moderate adductive tension and moderate medial compression . . . overall muscular tension throughout the vocal apparatus is neither high nor low. (Laver 1980:15)

Modal voice is considered unmarked and, in the Zaiwa data, it occurs in the majority of syllables.

3.4.5 The interaction of pitch and voice quality

Tone in Southeast Asia has taken on its own unique features which differ from tone elsewhere. Matisoff states that:

> The development of full-fledged tonal systems of the "omnisyllabic" type seems to be unique to East and Southeast Asia. In a language with an omnisyllabic tone system, virtually every syllable occurs

---

[28]The only nonsonorants that can occur in Zaiwa tense voice syllables are stops and affricates.

[29]Burling's creaky voice is actually tense voice.

[30]Naxi is a Tibeto-Burman language closely related to Zaiwa.

[31]Maddieson and Ladefoged (1985) make a tense/lax distinction for Jinghpaw and Wa due to initial consonant voicing changes and a tense/lax distinction for Yi and Hani from final consonant loss.

with a distinctive tone that is not predictable either in terms of the syntactic structure of its phrase or phonotactically in terms of neighboring syllables. These tones are not just oppositions of higher vs. lower pitch, but are complex bundles of prosodic features including pitch, contour, vowel length, and "phonation type" (clear, creaky, breathy voice). (1989a:147)

Tibeto-Burman languages in general, and Zaiwa in particular, are no exception to Matisoff's description. Voice quality differences correlate with tonal differences in many Tibeto-Burman languages (Glover 1971). Different languages exploit this interaction differently. Some Tibeto-Burman languages, such as Rawang, have tone, but no contrastive voice quality distinctions (Morse 1962:70). Some, such as Burmese, include voice quality as a part of the contrastive tone or register (Maran 1971:49).[32] Some languages, such as Zaiwa, have contrastive voice quality in nonchecked syllables and voice quality correlating with pitch height in checked syllables. Some languages, such as Maru, have contrastive voice quality with all tones in all syllable types. The full range of voice quality interaction with tone within the same language family reveals an underlying independence of pitch and voice quality with tendencies toward certain correlations.

The interaction of tone and voice quality depends on the state of the glottis. Both vocal fold tension and glottal aperture help to determine pitch with different phonation types. Vocal fold tension can affect pitch in the voiced, creaky, and tense phonation types by movement of the arytenoid cartilages or thyroid cartilage and by contraction of the vocal folds producing longitudinal tension. The arytenoid cartilages can move together or apart and can rotate to change vocal fold tension. The closer the arytenoid cartilages move together, the less tension there is on the vocal folds and the lower the pitch will be. This is apparent in creaky voice where arytenoid cartilages are adducted, and pitch is generally low. When the glottis is constricted, the vocal cords are lax unless the thyroid cartilage moves forward to stretch the glottis or the vocal folds contract and increase longitudinal tension, as occurs with tense voice. This raises the pitch (Ladefoged 1972:78).

The rate of vibration produced in various phonation types also depends partly on the size of the glottal aperture, which affects the subglottal pressure. Of the three laryngeal states of interest in this book, creaky voice ([+const vf], [−stiff vf]) is vibrated most easily, takes the least subglottal pressure, and has the lowest tone. Modal voiced segments ([−const vf], [−stiff vf]) have neutral subglottal pressure, and tone is

---

[32]The integration of tone, segmental type, and voice quality is so developed in Burmese that Bradley (1982) has presented an argument for calling Burmese a register language instead of a tonal language.

determined by surrounding segments and independent laryngeal controls. Tense voice segments ([+stiff vf]) have the most complete glottal closure, require the highest subglottal pressure to vibrate the vocal folds, and have a tendency towards higher tone. The closer and tighter the vocal folds are, the more subglottal pressure is needed to overcome the constriction or muscular tension and vibrate the vocal folds. An example of this is seen in Yi as presented by Maddieson and Ladefoged (1985). They state that Yi shows a slightly higher pitch on tense syllables in comparison to lax syllables. Tense vowels also correlate with greater respiratory effort and greater glottal constriction which produces greater subglottal pressure.

4
An Autosegmental Framework for the Analysis and Representation of Tone and Voice Quality in Zaiwa

As noted before, Zaiwa, like most Asian languages, shows interaction between the segments and suprasegments. But there are also some aspects of segmental analysis independent of the suprasegmentals (such as certain vowel alternations) and some aspects of suprasegmental analysis independent of the segmental system (such as certain types of tone sandhi). Many aspects of the segmental and suprasegmental phonology, however, cannot be understood without the other, such as the effect of voice quality on consonant voicing, and the influence of consonants on tonal variations. A framework for phonological analysis and representation is needed that allows for independent function of the segmental and suprasegmental systems, while also accounting for the interaction between the features of segments, tone, and voice quality. This chapter will define the prerequisites necessary to develop a framework for the representation of tone and voice quality in Zaiwa (§4.1), define the domains of tone and voice quality (§4.2), review previous representations of tone and voice quality which contribute to the system developed for this study (§4.3), and suggest a framework for the autosegmental representation of tone and voice quality in Zaiwa (§4.4).

4.1 Prerequisites to tonal representation

In this section some of the prerequisites to the development of a framework for the representation of tone will be discussed. The general differences between CONTOUR and REGISTER tone will be presented (§4.1.1), and the features which have been included with tone in Asian languages will be reviewed (§4.1.2). A topic specifically related to Zaiwa is also discussed in more detail: lexical tone versus derived tone (§4.1.3). The data introduced in §4.1.3 will be used as the raw material which will motivate the framework for tonal representation and voice quality in Zaiwa.

4.1.1 Contour and register tone

Tone can be either register tone, consisting of pitch spaces at different levels, or contour tone, which rises or falls as a unit. Tonal register, as used here, refers to the relative height of the pitch on a syllable in comparison with the overall tone space. Tonal contour refers to the shape or direction of movement of the pitch trajectory over the duration of the syllable.

Contour tones can be considered as a series of level tones or single unitary tones realized on a single TBU, just as a level tone is. In many tonal languages, especially those in Africa, there is evidence that contour tones should be considered a series of level tones. In fact, many tone scholars prior to the 1980s believed that there was very little evidence in any language that necessitated the representation of contour tones as a unit. Anderson (1978:160) concluded that "tonal glides are always to be represented as sequences of tone levels." Wang (1967), however, suggests that Asian tones are organized in a fundamentally different way than African tones in that Asian tones have unitary contours. More recently, Yip (1993) and others have argued for unitary contour tones in some Asian languages, especially dialects of Chinese, due to the fact that contour tones spread and reduplicate as units. The assignment of pitch contour as a series of level tones or as a unit depends on the assignment of tone to particular TBUs and tone sandhi interactions.

The nature of Zaiwa tones as unitary contours versus a series of register tones is not in focus in this thesis. Suffice it to say that Zaiwa has two contour tones (53 and 31) and one level tone (4). There is no overwhelming evidence in Zaiwa which would obviously necessitate representing contour tone as a series of level tones or as a unit. Downdrift, as defined by most linguists, does require a low tone following a high tone and may be used to argue for contour tones as a series of level tones in Zaiwa. In the absence of any further evidence, contour tones will be considered to be a series of level tones in Zaiwa. For example, 53 will be considered a high falling tone made up of a 5 followed by a 3.

4.1.2 Features included with tone

The question of which segmental and suprasegmental features to include with tone is determined language by language. Some linguists have analyzed voice quality and glottal plosive/restriction as part of the tone system in Tibeto-Burman languages. Glottal stop is included with the tone in Lahu (Matisoff 1973a:10). Creaky voice quality is included as a part of the tone #3 in Burmese.[33] Linking pitch and voice quality has been done where there are restrictions on occurrence between tone, voice quality, and final glottal plosive.

Benedict (1948), approaching the problem from a historical perspective, gives a warning concerning combining features:

> Tonal accents should be strictly distinguished from other suprasegmental features not directly related to pitch (glottalization, stress) as well as from segmental elements, including glottal stop....This failure to delimit tone has been responsible for much of the 'fuzzy' writing that has appeared on the tonal systems of this area. (1948:6)

Matisoff (1973a:25) comments that "There is no mechanical way to decide whether a syllable-final [ʔ] in a given Lolo-Burmese language is better to be regarded as a final consonant or as a tonal feature."

In Zaiwa, glottal plosives occur in all of the same environments as the oral plosives, in both tense and modal syllables. Glottal plosives and oral plosives both interact with pitch in checked syllables in a similar manner. Tense voice occurs with all contrastive tones in unchecked syllables. Tone and voice qualities are not linked in unchecked syllables and are not predictable from each other. Due to the parallel distribution of glottal plosives with oral plosives in relation to pitch and voice quality, and the full distribution of tense voice with all tones in Zaiwa, tone, tense voice, and final glottal plosive will be analyzed as separate phenomena.

4.1.3 Lexical and derived tone in Zaiwa

Zaiwa has both kinds of tonal prosodies, LEXICAL TONE and DERIVED TONE. Lexical tone is contrastive tone assigned at the level of the lexicon. It is not predictable. Derived tone, by contrast, is predictable from the segmental and suprasegmental features associated with the segments of the syllable. Derived tone is a natural, noncontrastive result of the phonological rules affecting the segmental and suprasegmental features of the syllable. In Zaiwa unchecked syllables, tone is assigned by associating lexically specified tone from an autosegmental tier to a TBU as expected. In checked syllables,

---

[33]Tone #3 is that tone often written in Burmese with a subscripted dot.

however, tone is derived by spreading previously associated glottal features to the vowel from the surrounding segments.

Zaiwa has three contrastive lexical tones:[34] high falling (53), high-mid level (4), and mid falling (31). In open syllables and in syllables closed by a nasal, all three tones can contrast irrespective of initial consonant voicing and voice quality as seen in (27).[35]

(27) a. [ʃɔ⁵³]   'tongue'   [ʃɔ⁴³.wṵi³²] 'bone'   [ʃɔ³¹]   'flesh'
      b. [mjaŋ⁵³.ɛ³²] 'about horses' [mjaŋ³.ɛ³]   'long time' [mjaŋ³¹.ɛ¹²] 'see'
      c. [nja̰m⁵³.ɛ³²] 'slow'   [na̰n³.ɛ³]   'shiver'   [mja̰ŋ³¹.ɛ¹²] 'tall'

Example (27a) shows that tone is fully contrastive in unchecked syllables with voiceless initials. Example (27b) shows that tone is fully contrastive in unchecked syllables with voiced initials. A comparison of rows (27b) and (27c) show that in unchecked syllables, tone is not dependent on voice quality.

In checked syllables the situation is very different. Tone in checked syllables is derived and is predictable from the voicing of the initial consonant (C_i), and the presence or absence of tense voice quality. If C_i is voiceless, then tone is short and high, with partial to no fall (55, 54). If C_i is voiced, then tone is short and mid, with partial to no fall (33, 32). If the syllable has the tense voice autosegment, [+stiff vf], then tone is short and high, with partial to no fall (55, 54), independent of C_i voicing. A syllable final stop -ʔ is the minimal environment allowing initial consonant voicing and tense voice quality to affect tone. Therefore, there are two allotones of a single tone, high-checked (realized as 55 or 54) and mid-checked (realized as 33 or 32). Examples of tone in checked syllables are shown in (28) and should be contrasted with (27).[36]

---

[34]Tone is represented in the phonetic transcription by tone numbers which were originally introduced by Chao (1930) as a "tone letter" system. For Zaiwa, five phonetic tone levels are distinguished with 5 as high, 4 as mid-high, 3 as mid, 2 as low-mid, and 1 as low. Contours are written as a combination of the beginning and ending points of the contour, e.g., 53 (high tone falling to mid tone). The same tone numbers are regularized and used to distinguish the three phonemic tones of Zaiwa (53, 44, 31), but the actual phonetic realization of each phonological tone can vary as shown in §6.1.

[35]A period in the phonetic transcription marks a syllable break. A + under a vowel indicates tense voice quality. The tones of word final particles will be discussed in §6.7 and are not in focus here.

[36]The perfective aspect particle /e/ is not included with the verbs in this section in order to show the processes more clearly and simply. The absence of the particle does not affect the derivation of tone.

An Autosegmental Framework

(28) [bɨk³²] 'shoot' [pʰɨk⁵⁴] 'trap fish' [pɨ̰k⁵⁴] 'kick'
[lɔʔ³²] 'hand' [sʊt⁵⁴] 'kill' [la̰p⁵] 'flash'
[nɪk³²] 'bamboo shoot'   [nɪ̰k⁵] 'heart'

It is clear that syllable type (CV, CVN, or CVS), voice quality ([+/−tense vf]), and voicing ([+/−voice]) all interact to determine tone in checked syllables. The data presented in (27) are used as examples to represent lexical tone, and the data in (28) will be used to help define a framework for the representation of tone and voice quality in Zaiwa. The framework to be developed will show that all of these interactions in checked syllables can be reduced to the spreading of glottal features from segments and autosegments to the glottal nodes of vowels. Underspecification and the feature geometry of the laryngeal node will be used to explain the interactions.

4.2 The domains of tone and voice quality

In order to develop a framework for the representation of tone and voice quality in Zaiwa, the domains of tone and voice quality must first be defined. The domains of tone and voice quality will determine the boundaries for lexical assignment and derivation. The segments in the domain will be the points of attachment for tone and voice quality assignment. A review of the domains of tone and voice quality in Tibeto-Burman languages will help to determine the domains of tone and voice quality in Zaiwa.

Tibeto-Burman tones are intricately and historically tied up in syllable structure. Tonogenesis in Tibeto-Burman languages is an excellent example of the interaction between the initial and final consonants of a syllable and their diachronic metamorphosis into tone on the syllable.[37] Benedict (1948:190) proposes the syllable as the prosodic unit for tone in Southeast Asian languages. Maran (1971:101) agrees stating that "the structural domain of ... 'tones' is the syllable, and the phonological rules operate on that domain." Morse (1962:68) states, "in the Burmic languages every syllable exhibits a single toneme, which is co-extensive with the syllable, its starting point co-occurring with onset of the initial and its end-point coincident with the final." In Zaiwa the domain of lexical tone is the syllable.[38]

---

[37]See Matisoff 1973b and Mazaudon 1976 for an introduction to Tibeto-Burman tonogenetics. See §3.4.3 for a discussion of the interaction between tone and features of phonological segments.

[38]The domain of tone and assignment of tone to a TBU are two different issues in this study. The domain of tone is defined by the boundaries within which tone has its primary phonetic manifestation, i.e., the syllable. The assignment of tone to a TBU is a more abstract phonological issue discussed in §4.4.2.

The next question is, what are the tone bearing units within the syllable? Yip (1993) reports that Duanmu argues for the mora as TBU, and indeed claims that there are two per syllable. Bimoraic syllables with obstruent codas are TBUs, but the absence of contour in syllables with obstruent codas is due to their being disallowed phonetically, while still present phonologically. She uses Duanmu's argument to argue for her own single root node model (see §4.3.4) in which the syllable is still the TBU, but contours are not realized in checked syllables due to phonetic factors. Yip (1995), based mostly on Chinese languages, seems to refine her definition of TBUs. She states,

> Some Chinese languages appear to use the mora, so that only long syllables may bear two tones, which surface as contours. However, I will adopt the view that the lack of contour tones on short syllables is a phonetic effect, and any syllable may phonologically bear any tone. It then follows that the TBU is the syllable, not the mora. (1995:476).

In contrast to her view, she reviews tonal representations presented by several different linguists. Hyman (1993),[39] Bao (1990), and Duanmu (1991) all propose the mora as the TBU, while Yip persists with the syllable. She also discusses the laryngeal/tonal connection between the final stops of checked syllables and tone stating that "These typically shorten the syllable, and often permit only level tones on the preceding vowel" (p. 487). In Chinese languages, sonorant-final syllables can bear any tone while obstruent-final syllables only bear shortened level tones. Yip (1995:488) explains these facts using the assumptions in (29).

(29) Contour tones have two tonal root nodes.
      The mora is the TBU.
      Only sonorant codas can be moraic.
      There is open syllable lengthening.

In her analysis, obstruent codas are nonmoraic and the single TBU of a checked syllable bears the tone of the first tonal root node.

In Zaiwa, all sonorant segments can carry pitch.[40] Pitch on a syllable actually begins with the first sonorant segment. However, a syllable initial sonorant or a sonorant in a consonant cluster, tend to be transitional elements for tone. At the beginning of an utterance or with words in isolation,

---
[39] Hyman (1993:77) states, "My claim is that tone, like other features, always targets the same landing site, the mora."

[40] In Zaiwa, pitch assignment is dependent on the voicing node of sonorants as discussed in §4.4.1. Obstruent voicing is derived from glottal features, and pitch is not assigned since there is no voicing node.

An Autosegmental Framework

a sonorant initial or a sonorant in a consonant cluster carry pitch from a neutral setting (3) to the starting point for the lexical tone. For example, the tone on an initial sonorant or sonorant in a consonant cluster is at level 3 or 4 preceding a 31 tone or 4 tone and goes from a 3 to a 5 preceding a 53 tone as shown in (30).

(30) CECIL tone trace plots of [gjɔ⁵³.ɛ³²] 'listen' and [gjɔ³.ɛ³] 'descend'

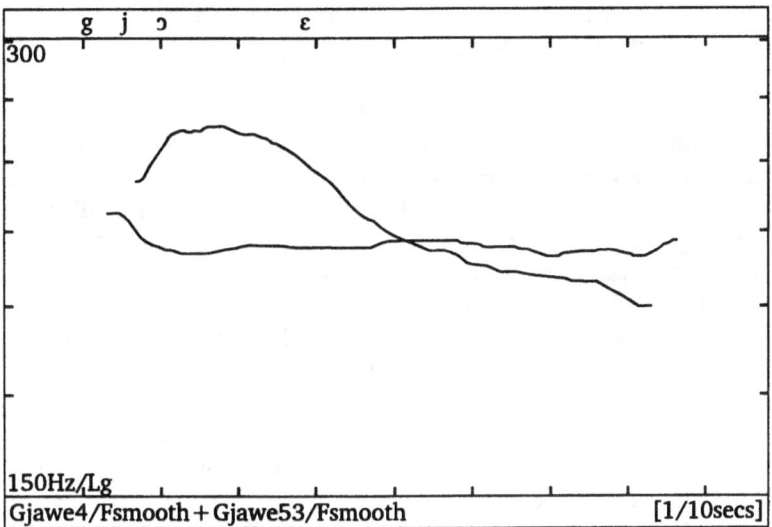

The tone on a Zaiwa syllable beginning with a voiceless obstruent begins at its initial lexical level on the vowel because there is no voicing over which it can be realized prior to the TBU. The tone pattern on a syllable beginning with a voiced obstruent is similar to the voiceless obstruent due to the extremely short duration of voicing. The tenseness of the vocal folds is most likely being adjusted during the articulation of the initial consonant or consonant cluster to the proper tension to create the assigned lexical tone. A sonorant initial, by contrast, allows this adjustment period to be heard, while an obstruent does not. The pitch on an initial sonorant or sonorant cluster may be involved in tone sandhi when utterance internal. Due to their transitional status, sonorant initials and syllable-initial sonorant clusters are not defined as TBUs.

Zaiwa TBUs are very similar to those proposed by Yip (1995): sonorant moras. The initial vowel is the location of initial tone association, and any additional lexical tones may be associated with any additional sonorant moras. With this definition, contour tones made up of two level tones may only associate with rhymes which have two moras. This includes CV:, CVV, and CVN syllables in Zaiwa.[41] According to CECIL calculations of tone length, the length of the lexical portion of tones in CV:, CVV, and CVN syllables is approximately equal (~200 ms or 100 ms for each mora). A CV syllable that precedes the obstruent onset of a following syllable is only approximately one-half as long as a CV: syllable in isolation or utterance finally, which contributes to tone shortening.

In Zaiwa, there is no need for a distinction between register and contour levels. It is not warranted by any phonological processes (chapter 6) and creates an unnecessary layer of representation. Pitch can therefore associate directly to the TBUs. It could be that in languages with both register and pitch, register has the syllable as TBU, and pitch has the mora.

The domain of voice quality in Zaiwa is the syllable. Most explanations of the origin of voice quality attribute it to either syllable-initial or syllable-final features of segments which in time became displaced, with the vowel being the carrier of the contrast (see §3.4.4). Tense voice quality in Zaiwa is likely a result of a preglottalized initial series in Proto-Tibeto-Burman (Burling 1967), the reduction of a historical *k to glottal stop, and possibly other processes which have not yet been determined.[42] Although the mechanism for this is not clear in Zaiwa, the origin of tense voice in syllables not ending in glottal stop is more likely due to features of historical initials than finals, since Zaiwa maintains a final stop and nasal series. All segments of a tense voice syllable are affected by tense voice and, therefore, can be regarded as tense voice bearing units. The initial consonant of the tense voice syllable will be the point of initial association of the tense voice quality autosegment ([+tense vf]) due to at least some historical evidence and convenience of spreading the feature from left to right.

4.3 Previous representations of tone and voice quality

Tone, voice quality, and their interaction have been discussed by numerous scholars. In this section the major proposals will be introduced and discussed in relation to their applicability to a framework for the representation of tone and voice quality in Zaiwa.

Voicing, pitch, glottal aperture, and vocal fold tension are the laryngeal features necessary to represent the interaction of tone with voice quality and segmental features in Zaiwa phonology. There have been many different attempts to represent tone using distinctive features and

---

[41]CV: is an open syllable with a long vowel, CVV is an open syllable with a diphthong rhyme, and CVN is a syllable closed by a nasal. Syllable structures will be discussed in §5.2.

[42]In a cursory comparison of Zaiwa tense syllables with Bradley's Proto-Lolo, tenseness in 7/23 syllables corresponded to *k → ʔ, 6/23 syllables corresponded to proto-preglottalized initials, and 10/23 did not have a clear correspondence with any proto-feature.

An Autosegmental Framework

feature geometry, and also a few attempts to include phonation type in the representation. A review of Halle and Stevens (1971), Duanmu (1991), Ladefoged (1989), and Yip (1989, 1995) will provide a background for discussing the features and framework necessary for a representation of tone and voice quality in Zaiwa.

4.3.1 The laryngeal feature system of Halle and Stevens

Halle and Stevens (1971) were the first to relate tone, voicing, aspiration, and voice quality using four distinctive features of the larynx. Their model uses the same features for tone, segments, and phonation types. The features proposed are [+/−spread glottis] and [+/−constricted glottis], referring to the aperture between the vocal folds, and [+/−stiff vocal folds] and [+/−slack vocal folds], referring to the tension or stiffness of the individual vocal folds. Each '+' feature is defined as a deviation from the neutral speech position. The table in (31) shows the application of the features to selected phonetic categories.

(31) Laryngeal features proposed by Halle and Stevens (1971)

	1	2	3	4	5	6
obstruents	b_1	b	p	p^h	ʔp	p'
glides	wy			hWY	ʔ	ʔ, ʔw
vowels	V	V (L)	V (H)		creaky vowels	glottalized vowels
spread glottis	−	−	−	+	−	−
constricted glottis	−	−	−	−	+	+
stiff vocal cords	−	−	+	+	−	+
slack vocal cords	−	+	−	−	+	−

Where: b_1 = lax, voiced stop, ʔ = slack glottal stop,[43] 1 = lax without tone affect, 2 = voiced with tone affect, 3 = voiceless with tone affect, 4 = voiceless aspirated, 5 = creaky (larygealized), 6 = glottalized (includes tense voice).

---

[43] A slack glottal stop allows a drop in pitch, approximating an incomplete glottal stop with slack vocal folds as found in creaky voice, while a stiff glottal stop tends to raise pitch and checks airflow.

Ladefoged (1973) adds co-articulated stop/glottal stop and tense voice to column six. The problem with Halle and Stevens' model is that in many languages tonal contrast, phonation type, and voicing are independent and, therefore, must be referred to by different features. The model also only provides for three levels of tone ([+stiff vf] [−slack vf], [−stiff vf] [+slack vf], [−stiff vf] [−slack vf]), which is insufficient for some languages with four or five level tones. Anderson (1978:164) notes that voicing could be considered to be based on either stiff/slack or spread/constricted, with not all features necessary. Anderson goes on to mention the widespread evidence that consonants influence tone, but the general lack of data that tone influences consonants. This asymmetry suggests some independence between the features of tone and consonant type. He concludes,

> It is entirely plausible to suggest ... that the gestures generally used to control voicing, aspiration, breathiness, laryngealization, etc., in consonants can have (unintended) consequences for the phonetic pitch contour, while the gestures used for primary pitch control have virtually no effect on the presence of voicing, etc. (1978:167)

This skewing suggests that Halle and Stevens' model of laryngeal features link different aspects of laryngeal production too closely.

4.3.2 Laryngeal feature geometry proposed by Duanmu

The representation of tone using feature geometry is not so straightforward. Pitch is primarily a product of the frequency of vibration of the vocal folds in the larynx. Therefore, pitch will come under the laryngeal node of the feature tree. Consonant voicing and phonation type interact with pitch and need to be integrated into the feature geometry in a way which shows their relationships. Sagey (1986, as reported by Duanmu 1991) uses the distinctive features of the larynx proposed by Halle and Stevens (1971) and applies them using feature geometry giving the structure shown in (32) (excluding features for aspiration).

(32)   laryngeal node

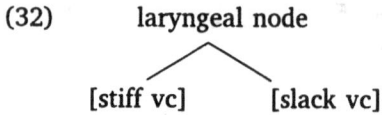

The features [stiff vc] and [slack vc] are used for both voicing and tone as shown in (33).

An Autosegmental Framework

(33)　　Feature　　　　　　　　　As voicing　　　　　As tone

　　a. [−stiff vc] [−slack vc]　　sonorant　　　　　　mid tone
　　b. [−stiff vc] [+slack vc]　　voiced obstruents　　low tone
　　c. [+stiff vc] [−slack vc]　　voiceless obstruents　high tone

When the features are applied to vowels, which are considered always voiced, the appropriate tone is produced. Obstruents are the only segments affected in relation to voicing, which is simply a matter of air pressure difference across the glottis. Obstruents have high supraglottal constriction which decreases airflow across the vocal folds. The low airflow is not enough to bring the vocal folds to oscillation if they are too tense. The reason vowels are not affected is that vowels have less supraglottal constriction allowing for greater airflow, which can overcome almost any degree of vocal cord tension (stiffness). Voicing is then a function of (1) supraglottal pressure, and (2) vocal fold stiffness and can be expressed by the features [+/−stiff vc] and [+/−slack vc] for each segment.

The problems with this model are that it only allows three levels for tone and it inherently associates obstruent voicing and tone, which is not always the case.

Duanmu went on to modify this geometry as shown in (34).

(34)　　laryngeal node

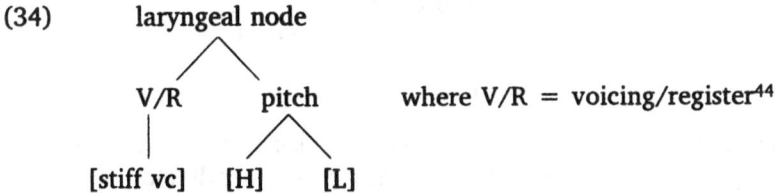

where V/R = voicing/register[44]

The feature [stiff vc] is used instead of [voice], where a [+stiff vc] is a voiceless obstruent, and consonant voicing is associated with tonal register. Tone is split into a register component and a pitch component, allowing six level tones ([+H] [−L], [−H] [−L], and [−H], [+L], each with a [+/−stiff vc] variant).[45] The voicing of sonorants is handled

---

[44]Duanmu and Yip define register differently. Duanmu (1991:142) defines register as "voice quality in the vowel that is ultimately related to onset voicing." Pitch does not play the major distinctive role. The use of the term in this way was first presented by Henderson (1952). Yip (1980) defines register as tonal levels corresponding to the traditional Chinese Yin and Yang registers. Register in the sense used by Duanmu is caused by a historical loss of voicing distinction which is replaced by a phonation type distinction and a change in vowel quality rather than tonal oppositions. The genesis of phonation type is commonly accompanied by pitch distinctions, but this is not universal (Mazaudon 1976:47).

[45]In this case there is overdifferentiation since no more than five level tones are attested in any language.

by underspecification. Duanmu (1991:149) suggests that "V/R correlates with vocal cord tension, and Pitch correlates with vocal cord thickness, via cricothyroid movement." Duanmu goes on to describe the phonetic correlate for V/R as voice quality and not F_0. Pitch on a vowel is marked on the pitch node with no marking on the V/R node if there is no marked voice quality due to underspecification. This representation has moreover the weakness that it associates pitch register with obstruent voicing at all times, which is not possible in Zaiwa.

4.3.3 Laryngeal feature geometry proposed by Ladefoged

Ladefoged (1989) proposed a laryngeal feature hierarchy distinguishing voice, glottal aperture, pitch,[46] and aspiration, as shown in (35).

(35)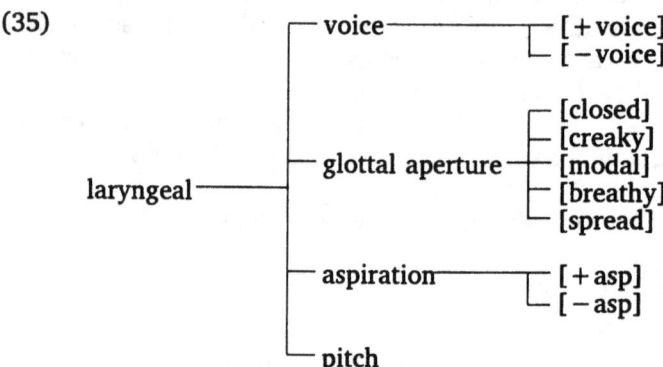

Ladefoged (1989:63) keeps voice and pitch separate because "in most tone languages both high and low tones occur in syllables with both voiced and voiceless consonants." This distinction is crucial for Zaiwa, though it differs from Halle and Stevens (1971), Duanmu (1991), and Yip (1995). Ladefoged's model is based on universal phonetic data and, therefore, not all aspects are necessary for Zaiwa. The model also does not capture any of the correlations between voicing, tone, and voice quality which are present in Zaiwa.

---

[46]Ladefoged did not elaborate on pitch apart from its place in the feature tree.

4.3.4 Tonal and laryngeal feature geometry proposed by Yip

Yip (1989) proposes a dominance model to capture the relationship between tone register and tone contour or pitch features and their relationships to various TBUs as shown in (36).

(36) Dominance

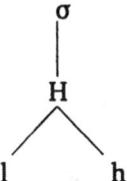

In Yip's dominance model, tone has its own root node attached to the syllable with the features [+/−upper] (indicated as H/L here), just as segments have a root node with the features [+/−son] and [+/−cons]. The root node dominates the contour features h/l ([+/− raised] in Yip's original representation). Yip shows that contour tones in Chinese languages spread as units and not as a series of level tones, which leads her to adopt her model. Yip (1995) shows that the only kind of tonal spreading which occurs is the spreading of terminal features (edge effects) and the spreading of the entire tone (unit replacement). Her model is restrictive enough to disallow other types of spreading while still allowing the types observed (register dominates pitch features, no special contour node).

Yip (1993:249) adapts her dominance model to account for phonation types as well. She states, "phonation differences frequently affect the observed pitch of the syllable, and behave phonologically in ways similar to tone." She then goes on to incorporate voicing distinctions with tone by adapting her 1989 tone model and equating register and obstruent voicing as suggested by Bao (1990) and Duanmu (1991)[47] as shown in (37).

(37)   σ
       |
       H/L   where H = [−voice] and L = [+voice] for obstruents
      / \
     h/l h/l

---

[47]Both Duanmu (1991) and Bao (1990) identify tone register with obstruent voicing. Bao uses the features [+/−stiff vocal cords] and Duanmu uses the features [+/−stiff] and [+/−slack].

Yip builds on their analyses and further separates her representation to include a register node, a pitch node, and a glottal aperture node, all dependent on the laryngeal node (38).

(38)

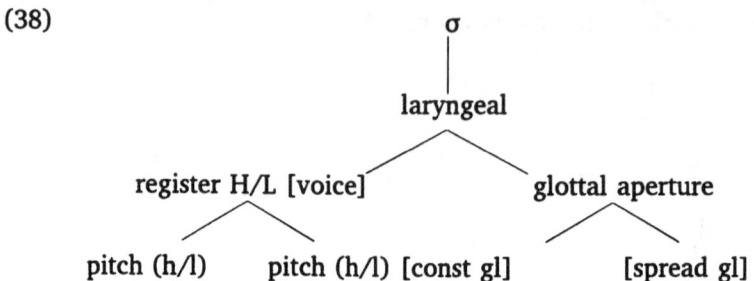

In this model, tone is closely linked with initial consonant voicing. This works for languages such as Shanghai (Yip 1993:249) in which initial consonant voicing always correlates with tone, but for languages such as Zaiwa, in which tone and initial consonant voicing only correlate in checked syllables, another model is necessary.

4.4 A framework for the autosegmental analysis and representation of tone and voice quality in Zaiwa

Each of the feature and feature geometry systems presented so far are either too narrow in their association of segmental features and phonation types with tone or too vague in their representation of the laryngeal features, not capturing the interactions which are possible. Tone is related to segmental features and phonation type in Zaiwa checked syllables and is lexically determined in Zaiwa unchecked syllables. Therefore, a framework for the analysis and representation of tone and voice quality will have to take all these factors into consideration, allowing the sharing of features between segments and suprasegmental properties when qualities overlap and keeping them independent when indicated.

In this section, the underspecification of features in combination with a feature geometry for Zaiwa will be proposed (§4.4.1). Next, the feature geometry will be employed in §4.2.2 to show how lexical tone will be represented in Zaiwa. Finally, the underspecification and feature geometry will be utilized to represent derived tone in both modal and tense syllables in §4.4.3.

An Autosegmental Framework

4.4.1 Underspecification and feature geometry for the representation of tone and voice quality in Zaiwa

In order to isolate syllables which manifest tone due to tonal derivation and syllables which are assigned a lexical tone, underspecification will be used in combination with feature geometry to represent the necessary conditions and environments.

The underspecification of segmental, tonal, and voice quality features in Zaiwa. In this section a combination of three of the laryngeal features proposed by Halle and Stevens (1971), [+/−spread], [+/−stiff], and [+/−const], and one added by Ladefoged (1989), [+/−voice], will be used.[48] The laryngeal features of segment classes and voice quality in Zaiwa are shown in (39).[49] Nonsonorants do not have a voicing node, as will be shown and, therefore, are not marked for [voice].

(39) The laryngeal features of segment classes and voice quality in Zaiwa

	[+son] tense voice	[−son] voiced	[−son] vl asp	[−son] vl unasp (tns voice)[50]	vl unasp stop$^?$,[51]?
voice	+					
stiff vf	−	+	−	+	+	−
const vf	−	+	−	−	+	+
spread vf| −	−	−	+	−	−

---

[48]The features [+/−stiff vf] and [+/−const vf] are used in underspecification to represent tense voice quality and glottal constriction, respectively. They are simply convenient phonological symbols to represent more complex states of the larynx. The actual phonetic correlates for tense voice and glottal constriction are more complex and are explained in §§3.4.4 and 6.8.

[49]Feature assignment to classes follows Halle and Stevens (1971). A glottal stop or glottal closure may theroetically be either [+const vf] or both [+const vf] and [+stiff vf]. The Zaiwa glottal stop allows some tone fall because air is allowed to leak through the glottis similar to a creaky glottal closure. A creaky glottal closure is [−stiff vf]. This leads to the assignment of [−stiff vf] for the Zaiwa stop$^?$ and ?. The feature values recorded here may not be universal for other languages due to the possible independent control of glottal features which can give nearly any combination of aperture, tension and sub-glottal pressure.

[50]Syllable-initial voiced obstruents become voiceless in tense syllables as discussed in §5.3.2. This process is restricted to voiced nonsonorants since [+spread vf] segments never initiate tense syllables. The features are redundant with tense voice, but are included here to clarify voicing on nonsonorants.

[51]Syllable-final voiceless stops are actually co-articulated stop$^?$ and are considered allophones of voiced stops in syllable-final position.

These features will be used to derive tone in checked syllables.[52]

Underspecification of the laryngeal features is useful in associating only the necessary contrastive features of the larynx to the segments so that the three glottal features involved in tonal derivation, [+/−stiff vf], [+/−const vf], and [+/−spread vf], can perform their phonological functions without interference from features which do not contrastively distinguish tonal or segmental differences. Underspecification also allows features to be associated with segments in unchecked syllables without an effect on tone. This underspecification can be represented as shown in the table in (40).

(40)

	[+son] tense voice	high-ckd tone	[−son] voiced vl unasp (tense voice)	[−son] vl asp	[−son] vl unasp stop?,?
voicing					
stiff vf	+	+			+
const vf		+	+		+
spread vf			+	+	

In (40), the voicing of sonorant segments is unspecified. Voicing of sonorants will be indicated by the presence of a voicing node in the feature geometry. The voicing of nonsonorant segments is unspecified and is predictable from the glottal features in (40). Therefore, the feature [+/−voice] becomes unnecessary. Notice that the high-checked tone (5, 54) has been added and specified by features of the glottal node. The mid-checked tone (3, 32) is unspecified and filled in by a default rule. The addition of the high-checked tone in (40) shows that the same features may be used for segments, tone, and voice quality in Zaiwa.

The high-checked tone is indicated by two sets of features shown in the chart which are associated to the same vowel. The glottal features [+stiff vf] and [+const vf] work in combination on a vowel to raise the frequency of vibration of the vocal folds and, therefore, raise pitch. See §3.4.5 for more details. The glottal features [+spread vf] and [+const vf] also work together to raise pitch, but in a slightly different manner than [+stiff vf] and [+const vf]. The pitch raising effect here depends to some extent on the Bernoulli effect as discussed in §3.4.4. It would seem that [+spread vf] and [+const vf] are mutually exclusive states of the glottis, but the combination of the two across a vowel, represents the rapid closure of the glottis when going from a [+spread vf] segment syllable initially to a [+const vf]

---

[52] A complete chart of distinctive features used in this study is found in appendix B.

An Autosegmental Framework 53

segment syllable finally. The [+spread vf] feature could be considered to be associated with the onset of the vowel, and the [+const vf] associated with the approach to the final consonant.[53]

In summary, the underspecification table in (40) shows the overlap between tone and glottal features in checked syllables and shows that voicing of stops is redundant with glottal features. The next step is to refine the laryngeal feature tree to allow for representation of all necessary features in checked syllables with minimal apparatus.

Feature geometry of the laryngeal node in Zaiwa. The feature geometry suggested by Halle (1992), as shown previously in (21), can be adapted and simplified for Zaiwa by changing the laryngeal node. Halle's glottal node is divided into a glottal node and a voicing node. The voicing node is added since voicing is not redundant with glottal features for all segments. [+/−spread vf], [+/−const vf], and [+/−stiff vf] are associated with the glottal node, and [pitch] values (5 4 3 1), are associated with the voicing node. [+/−slack vf] is not necessary since vocal fold tension does not necessarily correlate with voicing, and only two settings of tension are observed, which can be shown using [+/−stiff vf]. [+/−RTR] is also unnecessary and therefore deleted. The resulting feature geometry tree for the laryngeal node is shown in (41).

(41)   Feature geometry tree for the laryngeal node in Zaiwa

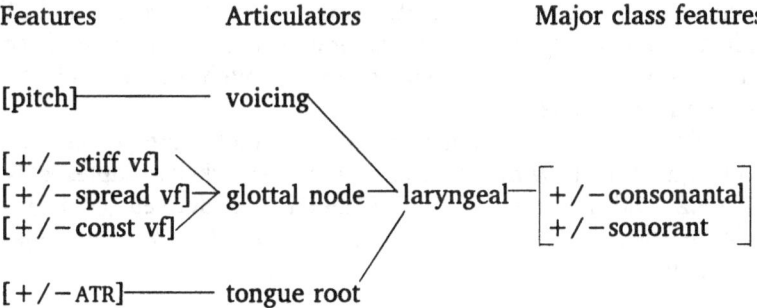

We will ignore the tongue root at this point since it is only referred to in vowel variations. Sonorant segments have the voicing and glottal nodes. Nonsonorant segments have only the glottal node since voicing is

---

[53][+spread vf] segments are also generally [+stiff vf] and both features may influence the rise in pitch. The choice of [+spread vf] as the distinctive feature for aspirated obstruents is based on the use of [+stiff vf] for tense voice quality. Separating [+spread vf] and [+stiff vf], and making each a distinctive feature in the underspecified representations, allows both to have a similar effect on pitch in checked syllables, but separates the features for tense voice and aspiration in unchecked syllables so that they can work independently.

redundant with glottal features. These facts give the feature geometry for sonorant segments shown in (42), and nonsonorant segments shown in (43).

(42) Feature geometry for the laryngeal node of sonorants

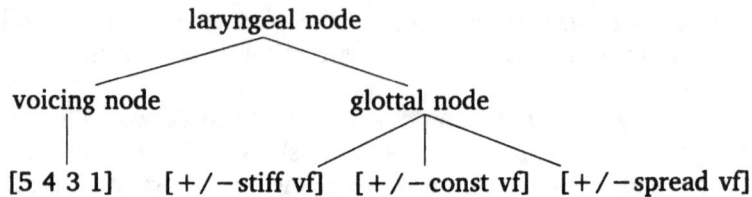

(43) Feature geometry for the laryngeal node of nonsonorants

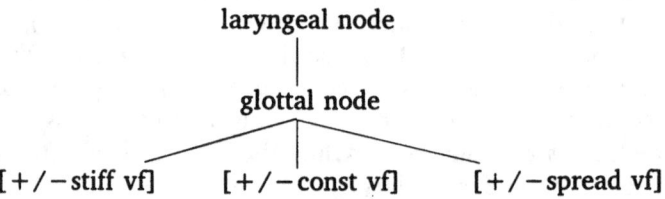

This feature geometry differs from those presented in §4.3 in that (1) consonant voicing, phonation type, and tone can be expressed independently or shown to correlate using underspecification, and (2) lexical pitch is dependent on the voicing node instead of the glottal features of the segments allowing independence of pitch and glottal features in unchecked syllables.

Using the proposed underspecification and feature geometry, it is now convenient to show how lexical tone in unchecked syllables is associated (§4.4.2) and how tone in checked syllables is derived (§4.4.3) based on glottal features of the segments surrounding the vowel nucleus and the voice quality.

4.4.2 The representation of lexical tone and voice quality in Zaiwa modal and tense voice syllables

Contour tones in Zaiwa are considered to be made of two level pitch units and not a single contour tone as discussed in §4.1.1. High falling tone (53) is represented as a high register tone (5) followed by a mid register tone (3), as shown in (44).

An Autosegmental Framework

(44)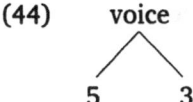

Mid falling tone (31) is represented as a mid register tone (3) followed by a low register tone (1), as shown in (45).

(45)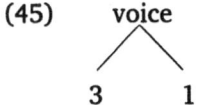

A high-mid level tone (4) is represented as a high-mid register tone (4) as shown in (46).

(46)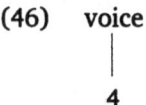

Each tone associates with a TBU, one to one, left to right, following the universal association convention in (20), as shown in (47).

(47) Lexical tone association for [bum^{31}] 'mountain'

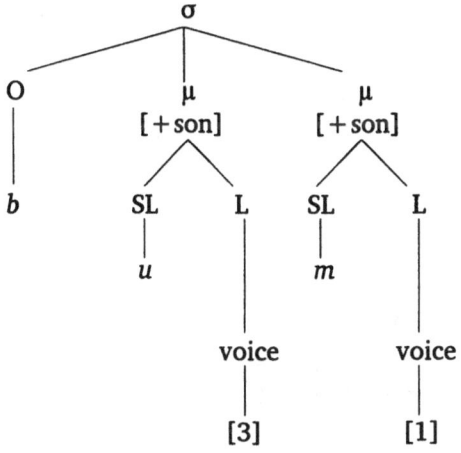

The feature geometry is simplified for the remainder of this study by merging the supralaryngeal and laryngeal nodes and excluding the redundant voice node for sonorant segments as shown in (48).

(48) Simplified lexical tone association for [bum³¹] 'mountain'

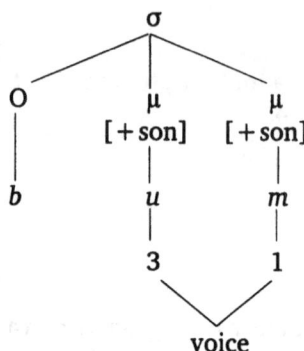

There is no association of features in the rhyme with the glottal aperture node or glottal tension node according to underspecification, so the nodes are left out for convenience.

If a TBU is left unassociated, then the last tone in the series spreads to the unassociated TBU. This occurs with the high-mid level tone as shown in (49).

(49) Lexical tone association for [mjin⁴] 'night'

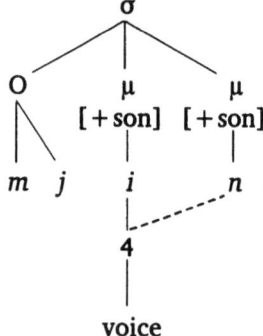

On bi-sonorant rhymes, the contour tone has full expression. This includes CV: syllables with a long vowel, which equals two moras as shown in (50).

(50) Lexical tone association for [wi:³¹] 'bamboo'

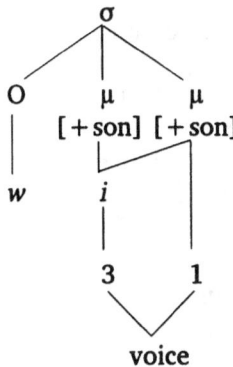

Lexical tone association for unchecked syllables with tense voice quality is shown in (51). Note that the tense voice autosegment is associated with the syllable onset and spreads to all voice quality bearing units, left to right, one to one, following the universal association convention.

(51) Lexical tone and voice quality association for [njąm⁵³] 'slow'

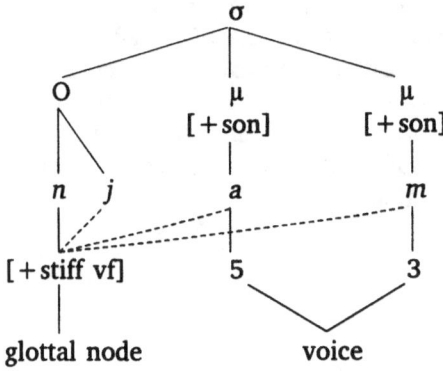

The environment for derived tone is never satisfied in unchecked syllables. The next section will discuss derived tone in checked syllables, which is not lexically associated.

4.4.3 The representation of derived tone and lexical voice quality in Zaiwa modal and tense voice checked syllables

The derivation of tone and association of voice quality in checked syllables will now be demonstrated step by step. The words with the initial consonants and voice qualities shown in (52) demonstrate all of the possible combinations of initial consonant types and voice qualities in checked syllables, thereby providing a representative sample of the observed interactions between tone, segmental features, and voice quality.

(52)

Initial consonant/VQ	Represents class	UF[54]	SF	
a. p^h	[−son], voiceless, aspirated	/p^hug/	[p^hɨk^{54}][55]	'trap fish'
b. b	[−son], modal voice	/bug/	[bɨk^{32}]	'shoot'
c. b, tense voice	[−son], tense voice	/bu̱g/	[pɨ̱k^{54}]	'kick'
d. n	[+son], modal voice	/nig/	[nɪk^{32}]	'bamboo shoot'
e. n, tense voice	[+son], tense voice	/ni̱g/	[nɪ̱k^{5}]	'heart'

A full derivation will be shown using the word /p^hug/ 'trap fish'. Portions of other derivations, for words (52b)–(52e), will be included and discussed at points where they differ and provide further insight.

The first step in tonal derivation is the assignment of the features from the table in (40) to the appropriate segments as shown in (53). The voicing node is left off of the sonorant segments since it is redundant and is not needed for tonal derivation.

---

[54]Notice that tone is not marked in the phonemic representation of checked syllables. Since tone is predictable, no overt reference is necessary. This would agree with Mazaudon's (1976) observation that Proto-Tibeto-Burman had a single tone in checked syllables. Also note that the final voiced plosive in the UF becomes a voiceless plosive in the surface form. This is discussed in appendix A.

[55]Vowel shape is due to an allophonic rule which changes /u/→ [ɨ] following a bilabial and preceding a velar. See appendix A for more details. The partially falling character of the tones in checked syllables will be discussed in §6.3.1.

An Autosegmental Framework

(53)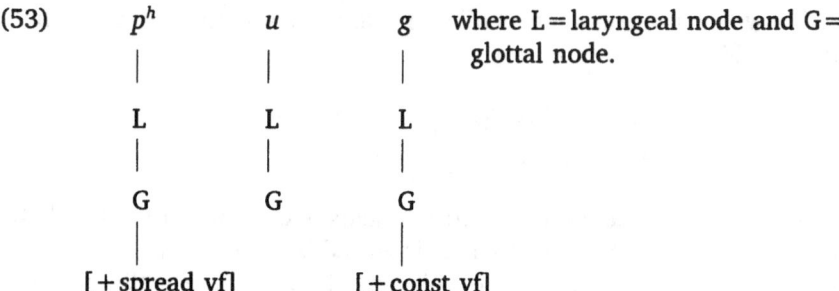

where L = laryngeal node and G = glottal node.

Next, the glottal features spread. The [+const vf] is spread from right to left to the empty glottal node of the preceding segment, which is always the vowel nucleus, as shown in (54). It does not spread any further since the only segment which is affected by the glottal closure is the immediately preceding vowel.

(54)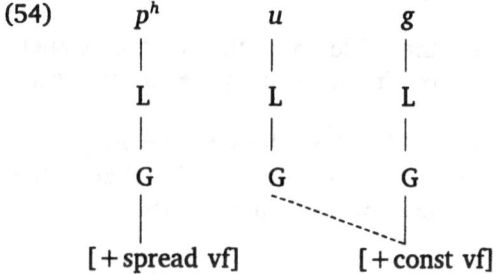

Following the spread of the glottal feature of the syllable-final consonant, the glottal feature [+spread vf], spreads from left to right, from the initial consonant to the vowel as shown in (55). The glottal feature [+spread vf] does not spread any further than the vowel since the beginning of the vowel is the extent of its influence.

(55)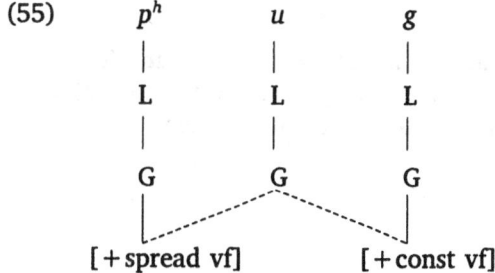

The glottal node of the nuclear vowel now satisfies the conditions to derive a high-checked tone, as shown in the table in (40).

The voicing of sonorants is filled in using the sonorant voicing default rule in (56).

(56)   Sonorant voicing default rule
       [+son] → [+voice]

The surface voicing for [−son] segments is determined by the glottal features. A [−stiff vf] nonsonorant is voiced. A [+stiff vf], [+const vf], or [+spread vf] nonsonorant is voiceless. This is phonetically plausible due to the fact that it is difficult to vibrate stiff, constricted, or spread vocal folds.[56] Phonetic redundancy rules for nonsonorant voicing are shown in (57).

(57)   Nonsonorant voicing redundancy rules
       [−stiff vf] → voiced
       [+stiff vf], [+const vf], or [+spread] → voiceless

Filling in phonetic tone from the table in (40), and the phonetic redundancy rules for nonsonorant voicing (57), gives the correct surface form [pʰɨk⁵⁴] 'trap fish'.

The derivation of the surface form for /bug/ 'shoot' following underlying feature association and spreading as demonstrated earlier in (53) and (54), respectively, gives the representation shown in (58).

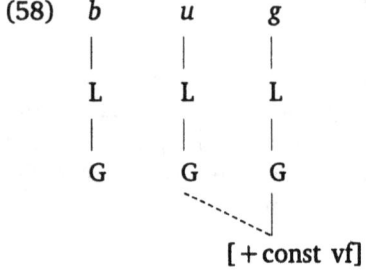

(58)   b   u   g
       | | |
       L   L   L
       | | |
       G   G   G
                  [+const vf]

The glottal node of the initial stop is not associated to any feature. A default rule is needed to assign the correct glottal feature. [−stiff vf] is the default glottal feature proposed here. The default rule for an empty glottal node is shown in (59).

---

[56]Obstruents are affected due to the high supraglottal pressure caused by oral closure, decreasing airflow to a level too low for focal fold vibration. Sonorants, however, have sufficient airflow to maintain voicing.

An Autosegmental Framework

(59) Empty glottal node default rule

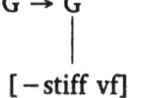

The [−stiff vf] feature is associated to the leftmost unassociated glottal node and spreads left to right to the available glottal nodes as shown in (60).

(60)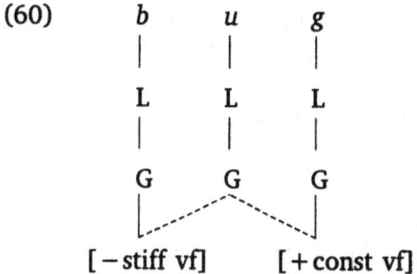

The glottal node of the nuclear vowel is now [−stiff vf], [+const vf], which is not a valid feature combination for a high-checked tone as shown in the table in (40). The default mid-checked tone rule (61) fills in the phonetic tone. This rule applies after all glottal features have applied and spreading is complete.

(61) Default mid-checked tone rule
    V → mid-checked tone
    |
    [−stiff vf]

Voicing is filled in by (56) and (57), giving the surface form [bɨk³²] 'shoot'.

The derivation of the word /bųg/ 'kick' starts with the association of features from the table in (40) and feature spreading (62). The feature [+stiff vf], which is the tense voice autosegment is associated with the first slot in the syllable, spreading left to right.

(62)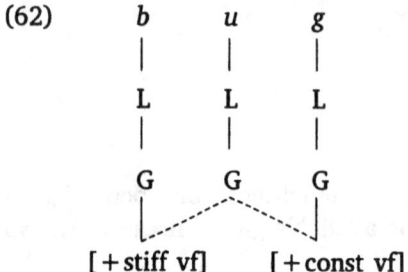

High-checked tone is assigned from (40), and the sonorant voicing default rule (56) and the empty glottal node default rule (57) are applied to give the surface form [pi̤k⁵⁴] 'kick'.

The rules used to derive tone and voicing for (52a), (52b), and (52c) are listed in (63).

(63) 1. Associate glottal features from (40).
2. Spread the glottal features to the vowel nucleus.
3. Apply sonorant voicing default rule (56) and empty glottal node default rule (59)
4. Assign phonetic tone based on glottal features in (40). If features for tone assignment are not associated with the vowel, apply the default mid-checked tone rule (61).
5. Assign phonetic voicing to nonsonorants based on nonsonorant voicing redundancy rules (57).

Sonorant initial checked syllables behave similarly to nonsonorant initial checked syllables. Rules (63) 1–4 apply to derive the correct surface structure for (52d), [nɪk³²] 'bamboo shoot', in (64).

(64)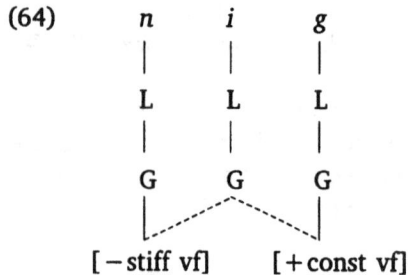

Rules (63) 1–4 are also applied to sonorant-initial syllables with tense voice quality as demonstrated with (52e), /ni̤g/ 'heart'. The correct surface form, [ni̤k⁵], is shown in (65).

An Autosegmental Framework

(65)

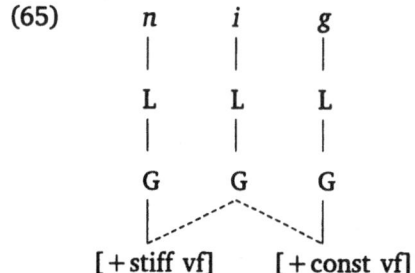

Comparing 'bamboo shoot' (64) and 'heart' (65) shows that sonorant voicing is not determined by features of the glottal node. (64) and (65) also show that voicing of the initial consonant is not a critical feature for determining tone height in checked syllables.

This section demonstrated the use of underspecification and feature geometry to show the interaction of tone, segmental features, and voice quality in checked syllables. The process by which surface tone is derived in checked syllables was shown step by step. The spreading of the glottal features [+/−stiff vf] and [+/−spread vf] in combination with [+/−const vf] were shown to be responsible for the determination of tone at the surface level in checked syllables. It was also shown that voicing correlates with glottal features in nonsonorant initials but is not a critical feature for tone assignment for syllables with sonorant initials.

5
Aspects of Zaiwa Segmental Phonology

In this chapter, a brief overview of Zaiwa segmental phonology will be presented. Aspects of Zaiwa segmental phonology which are relevant to the consideration of prosody, such as syllable structure, reduced syllables, and segmental phonological processes related to voice quality, will be discussed in more detail. Further aspects of Zaiwa segmental phonology are included in appendix A and have not been included here so that the theme of Zaiwa prosody would not be unduly interrupted.

5.1 The phonological word

Phonological features distinguish the phonological levels of Zaiwa speech from the paragraph down to the phoneme. Five levels of Zaiwa phonology can be distinguished: paragraph, breath group, word, syllable, and phoneme. Each level is distinguished by certain phonological features as summarized in (66).

(66) Phonological level   Phonological features

paragraph   intonational patterns, long pause, a rise at the end
breath group   stress (intonation), medium pause, and downdrift
word   segmental rules, stress patterns, tone interactions, minimal pause, and syllable structure
syllable   segmental and suprasegmental distribution
phoneme   distinctive features

Chapters 5 and 6 will discuss the phonology of the phonological word and below with some mention of breath groups in tonal processes.

The phonological word can be described in terms of the syllable combinations which occur. There are nuclear word slots with maximal substitutions allowed and peripheral affix or reduced slots with severely reduced substitutions allowed. Nuclear syllables of words carry full tonal contrast and are stressed, e.g., /mjin⁴/ 'night'. Peripheral syllables lack stress and have less distinctive or no tonal contrast, e.g., the first syllable in /lamʔ⁴/ [lə⁴.mʔ⁴] 'moon' is reduced and carries no lexical tone. Nuclear words may be made up of one to four syllables, but are generally restricted to one syllable for verbs and one or two syllables for nouns. Verbs of two or more syllables are generally a combination of noun–verb, noun–reduplicated verb, or negativizer–verb, e.g., /tsʰam⁵³dzen⁴e⁴/ 'hair^cut', /guŋ³¹tʃi⁵³tʃi⁵³e⁴/ 'body^bathe', /a³¹tʰɔʔ/ 'not^sharp (blunt)'. Verbs have both prefixes, which are limited to one per word, e.g., a negativizer, as shown above, and suffixes or particles indicating modality, directionality, and aspect, which can chain, e.g., /diŋ⁵³lɔ³¹e⁴/ 'close^motion away^perfective aspect'. Affixes on nouns are limited to suffixes marking case, possession, and number, e.g., /me³¹bu³¹be⁴le⁴/ 'clothes^plural^accusative'.

Words are also defined by word boundaries. Boundaries between words tend to have a slight pause allowing long vowels word finally. Syllable boundaries internal to words are marked by a short pause, stress, and tonal differences. Most phonological processes occur syllable internally or between syllable boundaries word internally.

5.2 Syllable structure

The Zaiwa syllable is the basic frame of reference for phonological description. The syllable is the smallest morphological unit, the domain of tone, voice quality, and stress, and the frame of reference for the distribution

Aspects of Zaiwa Segmental Phonology

of segments. The syllable is also the domain for several allophonic rules that make reference to syllable boundaries. In this section a traditional approach to syllable structure will be discussed, followed by a moraic approach with application to syllable weight. Finally, the distribution of syllable types and the structure of reduced syllables will be considered.

5.2.1 A traditional approach to syllable structure

Matisoff (1978:23) presents the traditional view of the Proto-Tibeto-Burman syllable canon as shown in (67).

(67) $(P)C_i(G)V(:)(C_f)(S)$

P is an optional historical prefix, C_i is the obligatory initial consonant, G is an optional second consonant /w j r l/ in a syllable-initial consonant cluster, V is the obligatory vowel nucleus, (:) is optional vowel length, C_f is the optional coda, and S is an optional suffix.

Bradley (1979:20) proposes a syllable structure more reflective of contemporary Tibeto-Burman syllables as shown in (68).

(68)   (Cə)C(C)V(C)T/R

The historical prefix interacted with the initial consonant and sometimes merged some of its features with C_i, resulting in the voicing of C_i. This helped to produce contrastive tone (T) and possibly voice register differences (R). In some cases the historical prefix remained basically intact with vowel reduction to a schwa and no contrastive tone as represented by the (Cə). The suffix is dropped in Bradley's syllable structure representation.

Zaiwa stressed syllables can be of six types: CV:, CVV, CCV:, CCVV, CVC, and CCVC. The V: is a long vowel while the VV represents a diphthong. Each syllable carries an obligatory tone and either modal or tense voice quality. The Zaiwa syllable can be either open or closed with the coda inventory limited to voiceless plosives and nasals. Syllable initial consonant clusters begin with plosives or nasals, and the second member of the cluster is either /j/ or /ɹ/. There is an unstressed CV syllable type generally restricted to reduced initial syllables, and an unstressed CV syllable restricted to verbal suffixes. These behave differently, as will be discussed in §§5.2.5 and 6.7. The Zaiwa syllable combines features of both the proposed Proto-Tibeto-Burman syllable canon (67) and the modern syllable canon (68) to give the syllable structure shown in (69).

(69)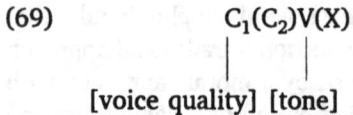

C_1 is the obligatory initial consonant, C_2 is an optional second consonant in a syllable initial consonant cluster, V is the obligatory vowel nucleus, and X is optional vowel length (:), the second member of a diphthong (V), or a final consonant (C_3).

A rhyme can consist of a long vowel, e.g., [aː], a diphthong, e.g., [ai], or a VC_3 combination, e.g., [an]. The obligatory tone and voice quality are suprasegmental features residing on separate autosegmental tiers. Voice quality is most obviously heard on the vowel nucleus, but it affects all members of the syllable. Diachronically, Burling (1967) identifies tense voice[57] as an artifact of preglottalized initial consonants. Whether preglottalized initials are the actual origin of tense voice in Zaiwa or not is still being debated. The association of voice quality with the initial consonant, however, provides a reasonable hypothesis about the nature of spreading of tense voice on an autosegmental tier to the segments in the syllable, and this procedure will be used here instead of initial association with the vowel to allow for a simpler synchronic analysis.

The CV: syllable is the minimal syllable type for stressed syllables. Note the examples of each stressed syllable type shown in (70).[58]

(70) CV: [pɔ̰³¹]   'frog'   [wa³¹]   'bamboo'
      CCV: [kʰjɔ⁵³]   'road, path'   [bjɔ³¹]   'bee'
      CVV   [bui³¹]   'sun'   [mau³¹]   'rain'
      CCVV   [gɹai³²]   'very'   [mə³.gui⁴.gjui⁴³]   'elephant tusk'
      CVC   [tʃʰaŋ³¹]   'ginger'   [ʔṵt⁵]   'gong'
      CCVC   [mjɨn³⁴]   'night'   [mjṵk⁵⁴]   'bury'

I assume that glottal stop is a syllable-initial consonant although it does not contrast with its absence syllable initially. The reasons for including glottal stop in the syllable-initial consonant inventory are that (1) glottal stop is a member of the segmental phonemic inventory and is not included as a product of tone or phonation type, (2) glottal stop is always heard preceding a vowel if no other consonant is present word initially and preceding a vowel following a CV syllable word internally, and (3) glottal stop

---

[57] Burling refers to creaky voice, which corresponds to the use of tense voice in this study.

[58] A note concerning phonetic transcription: All vowels in open syllables which are not [ə] are considered underlyingly long.

patterns with other stops syllable finally and is contrastive with its absence syllable finally, as shown in (71).

(71) [wɔʔ³².ɛ³]   'weave bamboo'   [wɔ³.ɛ³]   'have'
     [dʑɔʔ⁵⁴.ɛ²¹] 'boil'   [dʑɔ⁵³.ɛ³¹] 'correct'
     [guʔ³¹]   'paddy rice'   [gu³¹]   'younger sibling'

Excluding glottal stop from the inventory of syllable-initial consonants would increase the number of syllable types by three, adding V, VC, and VV, and make the analysis more complex.

Before proceeding further, an introduction to Zaiwa word-level stress is appropriate since stress is relevant in determining syllable structure. Stress is manifest as acoustic intensity, full vowel quality, and vowel length and does not necessarily correspond to pitch.[59] Zaiwa stressed syllables are the unmarked case. Unstressed syllables are the marked case, occurring with peripheral syllables, and show vowel shortening and vowel reduction to [ə] word initially and word internally. Suffixes generally occur as unstressed syllables, but the vowel is not reduced.

The P and S in the Proto-Tibeto-Burman syllable canon (67), and the (Cə) in Bradley's modern Tibeto-Burman syllable canon (68), have corresponding structures in Zaiwa. The P is actually a historical CV: prefix which, if present and unmerged with the initial consonant, is unstressed and generally no longer productive. The vowel is shortened and reduced to [ə], which gives a surface syllable structure of Cə in initial syllables of many modern Tibeto-Burman languages. The S is realized in Zaiwa as a CV: suffix when pronounced in isolation and always occurs as an unstressed syllable clause finally.[60] When S has a [ʔ] as C_1, the [ʔ] is deleted when the suffix is attached to a stem giving an atypical V syllable type. Examples of the atypical syllable types are shown in (72).

(72) Cə [ʔə³.kʰu⁵³.ɛ²¹] 'pinch off'   [lə³.ban⁵³.bɔ²¹] 'kapok'
     V   [kʰjup⁵⁴.ɛ²¹]   'sew'   [lai⁵¹.ɛ¹]   'pass'

In short, Proto-Tibeto-Burman P and S in Zaiwa are atrophied to a large degree.

---

[59] See §6.7 for the stress type that does affect pitch.

[60] The vowel of the unstressed suffix is not shortened in this case. Zaiwa is an SOV language and the final vowel suffix generally has no following segment in close juncture and, therefore, no shortening.

5.2.2 A moraic approach to syllable structure

In this section syllable structure will be represented in a moraic framework, with discussion of sonority constraints on syllable structure following aspects of Zec (1995). The moraic structure of the syllable will be analyzed and onset interaction with syllable weight will be discussed.

Zec identifies three sonority classes which help to differentiate syllable constituents and moraic structure. The classes assume an implicational hierarchy in which each lower class includes the class above it. Each class is distinguished by a major class feature as shown in (73).

(73)   a. [−cons]   vowels
       b. [+son]   vowels + sonorants
       c. ──────   all segments

Zec has shown that cross-linguistically, syllabic and moraic segments may belong to different sonority classes. The sonority of the syllabic segments is equal to or greater than the sonority of the moraic segments. Three classes of segments can be identified in Zaiwa based on sonority. The three classes can be important in determining domains of syllabicity, tone carrying ability, and moraicity. Zaiwa sonority classes are shown in (74).

(74)   Sonority class   Prosodic correspondence

       a. [−cons]   vowels   corresponds to syllabicity
       b. [+son]   sonorants   corresponds to tone carrying ability
       c. ──────   all segments corresponds to moraicity

In Zaiwa, only vowels are syllabic. Nasals can be syllabic in words borrowed from Jinghpaw, e.g., [n̩.duŋ³².ʃi²¹] 'jackfruit', but such examples are rare. This leads to the syllabicity constraint shown in (75).

(75)   Zaiwa syllabicity constraint

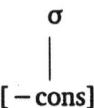

Heavy and light syllables in Zaiwa correspond to stressed and unstressed syllables, respectively. Stress in Zaiwa is limited to rhymes with either two vowel place slots (i.e., long vowels and diphthongs) or a single vowel place slot and a consonantal coda. These syllables are defined as heavy with each

Aspects of Zaiwa Segmental Phonology

position in the rhyme assigned a mora. Structurally more complex rhymes (VVC) are not observed. This constraint is manifested in the fact that vowel diphthongs cannot occur in closed syllables. Each member of a diphthong is a single mora, giving a maximal bimoraic structure for open syllables. An additional final consonant would add a third mora, which is not observed in Zaiwa. These observations lead me to postulate the bimoraicity constraint for Zaiwa in (76).

(76) Zaiwa bimoraicity constraint: A Zaiwa syllable may have at most two moras.

Cə and V syllables are unstressed (light) and are associated with only one mora. Vowels in closed syllables are inherently short and only act as a single mora with the second mora associated with the consonant coda. From this discussion it is clear that the first mora in the Zaiwa stressed syllable is filled by a vowel and the second by either a second vocalic segment (second member of a diphthong or second half of a long vowel), or by a final consonant. The final consonant (stop or nasal) carries weight and is moraic as shown by stress placement and the proscription on a final consonant occurring following diphthongs. Therefore, all segments which occur in the rhyme are moraic in Zaiwa. The Zaiwa moraicity constraint is represented in (77).

(77) Zaiwa moraicity constraint

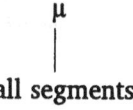

all segments

The relationship between stress and syllable weight can be stated explicitly as in (78).

(78) $[+\text{stress}] = \mu\mu$
$[-\text{stress}] = \mu$

Within the Zaiwa rhyme, there are constraints on moraic structure. The first mora of a syllable must be of equal or greater sonority than the second mora as represented in (79).

(79) μ μ
  | |
  r_i r_j where: sonority $(r_i) \geq$ sonority (r_j)

This constraint on moraic structure is generally applicable to the diphthongs /ai ui au ɔi/ as well, with the following sonority scale indicated: a, ɔ > u, i.

From the preceding discussion, the syllable structure can more accurately be represented as in (80).

(80)
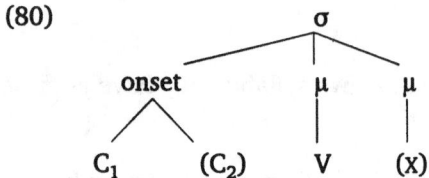

The specific allowed syllable structures for bimoraic, stressed syllables (heavy syllables) is represented in (81).

(81)
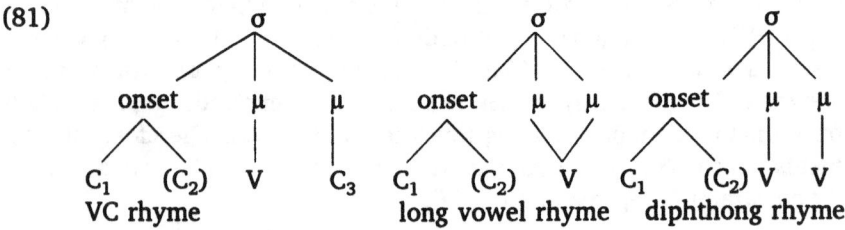

Notice that long vowels are represented as a vowel sharing two moras while diphthongs are represented as two vowels, each with its own mora.

The syllable structure for monomoraic, unstressed syllables is shown in (82).

(82)
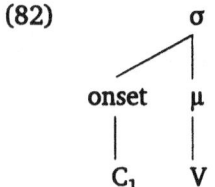

5.2.3 Syllable onset and syllable weight

In this section the interaction of the second member of consonant clusters with the rhyme is discussed. In particular, the effect of the syllable onset on syllable weight is considered.

The second consonant (C_2) of a consonant cluster is included as an optional part of the syllable onset in (80). There is, however, a possibility that certain onsets, and the second member of consonant clusters in

Aspects of Zaiwa Segmental Phonology

particular, may also contribute to syllable weight. Traditionally, Chinese linguists have captured this possibility by dividing the syllable into an initial consonant ONSET and a RHYME, consisting of the RHYME HEAD, RHYME ABDOMEN (nucleus), and RHYME TAIL (coda), as shown in (83), (L. Diehl, oral communication).[61] Chao (1968) describes the three constituents of the rhyme in Mandarin as a MEDIAL (semi-vowel), NUCLEAR VOWEL (head vowel), and an ENDING (nasal, i, u). What is commonly termed the second member of a consonant cluster such as /w j/ would be the head of the rhyme in this Chinese framework.

(83)

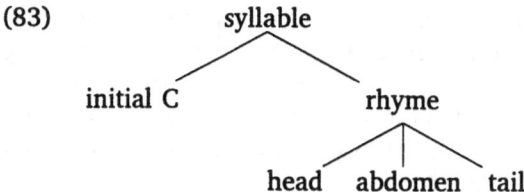

In Zaiwa the second member of an onset consonant cluster does not generally contribute to syllable weight. A complex onset can precede a bimoraic rhyme and still conform to the Zaiwa bimoraicity constraint, showing that the second member of the initial consonant cluster does not contribute to the weight of the rhyme, e.g., [bjɔm⁵².ɛ²] 'float'. In certain instances, however, the second member of an initial consonant cluster may contribute to syllable weight. Consonant clusters precede all types of heavy syllable rhymes (V:, VC, and VV). If the second consonant of an initial consonant cluster contributed to weight in these instances, then there would be two possible results, either (1) the sequence would produce a trimoraic rhyme, or (2) the rhyme would have to resyllabify into two syllables in order to maintain a bimoraic structure. The latter process seems to occur in Zaiwa in a limited environment.

Consider the diphthong /ui/, which is the only diphthong that occurs following /j/, /tʃʰ/, and /dʒ/. This restriction may be generalized to following /j/ if the affricates /tʃʰ/ and /dʒ/ are reinterpreted as /tʰj/ and /dj/, respectively.[62] Following /j/, the diphthong /ui/ becomes bisyllabic and is

---

[61]Diehl represents the basic structure as (x (x, x, x)) with the head, nucleus, and tail having equal status. He then makes two further distinctions based on a Northern (Mandarin) and Southern (Cantonese or Southeast Asian) distinction in languages. The Mandarin syllable type is represented as (x (x ((x)x))) with the coda more closely associated with the nucleus than the head. The Southeast Asian syllable type, of which Tibeto-Burman languages are considered a part, has the structure (x (((x)x)x)), where the head is actually the nuclear element and the abdomen and tail are, respectively, less closely associated with the head.

[62]/j/ follows all stops except /tʰ/ and /d/. The only alveopalatal affricates present in Zaiwa are /tʃʰ/ and /dʒ/. A reinterpretation of /tʃʰ/ and /dʒ/ as /tʰj/ and /dj/, respectively, may be indicated by the distribution. This will be discussed in more detail in §5.5.

reinterpreted as the sequence /u$i/[63] by the rule CjVV → CjV.V. For example, [pʰuŋ.tʃʰu.i] 'sugar cane' and [mə.gui.gju.i] 'elephant tusk', split the diphthong into two syllables. The motivation seems to be the weight contributed to the rhyme by the palatal glide preceding the diphthong. The glide has vocalic (syllabic) characteristics which push into the first mora adding additional weight and forcing the rhyme to give way to a new syllable. Instead of allowing a trimoraic syllable, which would break the bimoraicity constraint, Zaiwa reinterprets the diphthong as bisyllabic. The monosyllabic integrity of the diphthong can still be observed in syllables without a /j/ preceding /ui/, e.g., [dui³⁴] 'leaf raincoat', and in syllables with a /j/ preceding /ui/ in fast speech, word internally, e.g., [tʃʰui³².mɔ³.mi³²] 'widow'. In this case vowel shortening occurs allowing three 'vowel-like' elements to take up two moraic spaces. The absence of other diphthongs following palatal consonants may indicate their inability to become bisyllabic or may indicate the historical reduction of a /Cju.wi/ bisyllable to a /Cjui/ monosyllable.

5.2.4 Zaiwa syllable distribution

Given that Zaiwa morphemes are generally one syllable long, morpheme boundaries and syllable boundaries tend to coincide. Words of two to four syllables do occur, however, and are generally compounded words, which are derived from underlying monosyllables that retain part or all of their original meaning, e.g., /bjɔ³¹ʃum³¹mi³¹dziŋ⁵³/ 'bee^house^fire^point (candle)'. The percentage of each syllable type in monosyllabic and polysyllabic words is shown in (84).[64]

(84)

	Monosyllabic word	Polysyllabic word
CV	33%	43%
CCV	13%	6%
CVC	45%	44%
CCVC	9%	6%

CVC is the most common syllable type, followed by CV. The comparison of syllable types that occur in monosyllabic and polysyllabic words shows one interesting difference. The percentage of CV syllables in polysyllabic words goes up and the percentage of syllables beginning with CC clusters in polysyllabic words goes down. This is most likely due to the frequent

---

[63]/ui/ may also be reinterpreted as /u.wi/, maintaining a CV structure for the reinterpreted second syllable.

[64]In this case V is any vowel or diphthong in open syllables and a nondiphthong in closed syllables. Verbal suffixes were not included in the syllable count.

presence of initial CV reduced syllables in polysyllabic words, many of which came from historical CCV (C) syllables that have undergone vowel epenthesis to give modern Cə.CV (C) syllable types. This process will be discussed in the next section.

5.2.5 Reduced syllables

Reduced or weak syllables are common in Tibeto-Burman languages and have been the subject of extensive discussion, both historically and synchronically. The distinctive characteristics are that they never occur apart from a word, are toneless,[65] have a non-distinctive vowel, and carry less stress than neighboring syllables (Mazaudon 1976:79).[66] Reduced syllables, in combination with a full syllable, are described by Matisoff (1989:165) as "sesquisyllabic: a 'syllable and a half' long."

The origin of the reduced syllables has been widely discussed in the literature on Tibeto-Burman languages. One explanation for modern reduced syllables is a historical prefix system. Bradley (1971:2) writes that "Benedict has considered further data in reconstructing a Tibeto-Burman prefix system containing b d g r s ʔ m and rarely l"[67] and "It is assumed that the prefixes were atonal and [had a] schwa vowel; perhaps they originated from reduced forms of words, as the later BL [Burmese-Lolo] prefixes clearly did. It is usually assumed that BL has lost the TB prefixes."[68] Some of the specific historical prefixes, however, have been maintained. Benedict (1972:§28) posits a single Tibeto-Burman [ʔa] prefix which varies in phonetic manifestation depending on stress. The stressed prefix is pronominal and is used preceding kinship morphemes. The unstressed prefix is nonpronominal and is realized as [ʔə] ~ [ʔa].[69] The [ʔə] is used by Burmese to derive nouns from adjectives (Lehman 1975:37). Lehman notes that [ka-], [a-], and [na-] appear as reduced pronominal clitics in Tibeto-Burman and as possessive pronouns before nouns (p. 26).

---

[65] I assume that what Mazaudon means by 'toneless' is that the reduced syllables have no lexical or contrastive tone. Bradley (1982) states that the "minor syllable" does not occur with suprasegmentals in Burmese. Matisoff (1974:160) denies that there is tone on Jinghpaw unstressed prefixes.

[66] The Zaiwa reduced syllable is parallel to the structure of reduced syllables in Burmese (Cornyn 1944:7). Benedict (1948:188) describes the syllable in Burmese as an "atonal, nonfinal, 'reduced' syllable, with weak stress and centralized vowel."

[67] In this case, [ʔ] is the same as [ʔa] described by Wolfenden (1929). The [g], and supposedly the other voiced plosives, correspond to the voiceless counterparts (in specific languages, such as Kachin, presented by Wolfenden (1929:71).)

[68] The remnants of the prefixes can be seen in some languages as part of the initials or as part of tonal developments.

[69] The pronominal and nonpronominal [ʔa] prefixes in Tibeto-Burman were first discussed by Wolfenden (1929). He suggested that they were two separate prefixes.

There are, however, other sources for reduced syllables in addition to reduced historical prefixes. Matisoff (1989a:163) states, concerning Tibeto-Burman, that "a modifying syllable in a lexical compound may undergo such radical phonological reduction that its original morphemic identity is obscured. Once this happens, it can become more like a meaningless affix or 'formative' than like a full noun or verb." He goes on to describe three sources of reduced syllables in Jinghpaw: (1) historically recent additions to the root with no traceable meaning, (2) reductions of semantically obscure but fully syllabic prefixes, and (3) reductions of historically initial constituents in compounds which were once fully syllabic. Morse (1962:65) describes the vowel or reduced syllables in Rawang diachronically as an insertion coming from original consonant cluster prefixes of Proto-Tibetan and states that in many languages it is interpreted as a nonphonemic offglide between two consonants in syllable-initial position. Maran (1971:151) describes two types of syllable reduction for Burmese. The first involves prefixation; "In general, prefixation involves the reduction of the first member of a compound to its initial and an unstressed vowel." The prefix "has no distinct phonetic tone" (p. 158). The second is described as "another class of polysyllables which cannot be shown to be productively derived, these are bound forms where the prefixes are no longer clear as to what their original lexical meanings were" (p. 156). Mazaudon (1976:85) attributes some of the weak syllables in Burmese as coming from reduced morphemes while others came from vowel epenthesis between initial consonant clusters in Proto-Tibeto-Burman. Hongkai differentiates between prefixes and the Cə derived from historical consonant clusters:

> The historical behavior of prefixes is not quite the same as that of elements in true consonant clusters. In certain modern languages, the distinction between true prefixes and prefixal syllables which have come from the split up of consonant clusters is clear: the former often have an obvious grammatical meaning; the latter do not. The former are comparatively productive, often serving to put a word into a different form class. The latter do not behave this way. (1986:12)

Hongkai gives one excellent criteria for distinguishing the two types of reduced syllables: the remnants of historical prefixes should still be productive, while the prefix-type syllables resulting from vowel epenthesis between the consonants of a consonant cluster are not.

Zaiwa has unstressed, reduced syllables with a tendency towards vowel reduction to [ə]. The reduced syllable is always underlyingly open[70] and never carries tense voice quality. Zaiwa seems to have both productive, reduced syllables resulting from the reduction of historical prefixes

---

[70]The Cə syllable can be closed by a morphophonemic epenthesis process which adds a [t] preceding a [+cor], [+ant] consonant as discussed in appendix A, §A.7.

Aspects of Zaiwa Segmental Phonology 77

beginning with /b d g l m s ʔ/, as suggested by Benedict, and reduced syllables which are not productive and supposedly products of vowel epenthesis in historical consonant clusters.[71] Zaiwa also seems to have synchronic initial syllable reduction, with word-initial syllables not included in Benedict's proto-prefixes, but which reduce when unstressed. The vowels /a i u ɔ/ all can undergo this synchronic reduction to [ə]. This form of reduction follows the typical iambic rhythm meter seen in Asian light/heavy syllables sequences (L. Diehl, personal communication). If the "normal," productive, stressed synchronic prefix and "normal," stressed CV: syllables are added, there are a total of six CV syllable types in initial position. The table in (85) gives the syllable types, stress assignment, source, and examples of each.

(85)   Word initial CV syllable types

Syllable type	Stress assignment	Source	Examples	
CV:	stressed	"normal" (compound)	[ʔi³.ʃi⁵³] [lɔ³ʔ.jɔ³¹]	'urine' 'rightside'
CV:	stressed	"normal" prefix (productive)	[ʔa³.dʒɔ³¹]	'not correct (negative pre)'
CV:	stressed	historical prefix (productive)	[ʔa⁴⁵.ma⁵³ŋ]	'elder sibling (kinship pre)'
CV ~ Cə	unstressed	"syn reduction" (compound, prefix)	[ʃi⁴³.ɛ³] [ʃə⁴.bjɔ⁵¹]	'die' 'ghost (dead person)'
CV ~ Cə	unstressed	historically reduced prefix (productive)[72]	[kʰə⁴³.mjɔ̰³¹] [kʰa⁴.ju³²ʔ]	'how many (interrog. pre)' 'who'
Cə	unstressed	historical CC with vowel epenthesis	[73]	

Reduced syllables resulting from historically reduced prefixes and vowel epenthesis seem to be lexically toneless and tend to assimilate to the pitch trajectory of the following tone, which distinguishes them from

---

[71]An additional option is historical prefixes which have been reduced and are no longer productive.

[72]Following Benedict's proto-prefixes and their voiceless counterparts.

[73]This category is a bit contrived in the sense that all nonproductive cases of word-initial syllable production may fit here. There is no way to tell which cases are actually epenthetic and which cases are simply reduced productive prefixes without having sufficient historical data to verify their identities.

a normal stressed CV: word-initial syllable which carries contrastive tone.[74] This will be discussed more in §6.2.

Although there seem to be six underlying word-initial syllable types, they can be reduced to three surface forms: (1) CV syllables with nonreduced vowel and contrastive tone, (2) CV syllables with a tendency toward vowel reduction and contrastive tone, and (3) syllables with a reduced vowel and noncontrastive tone. The difference between the two types of vowel reduction is due to two different processes.[75] The word-initial CV vowel reduction with contrastive tone is most likely derived synchronically from a simple phonological process related to loss of stress due to syllable-initial position in the word as shown in (86).

(86) /ʃi⁴.bjɔ⁵³/ → [ʃə⁴.bjɔ⁵¹]   'ghost/(dead^person)'
         |
       [−stress]

The unstressed, reduced syllables with noncontrastive tone are either a product of historical vowel epenthesis, as shown in (87), or derivational morphology arising from typical productive compounding processes with diachronic syllable reduction resulting in unstressed derivational presyllables, as shown in (88).[76]

(87) CCV(C) → Cə.CV(C)
      vowel epenthesis

(88) kʰa⁴   + mjɔ̰³¹ →   kʰə⁴.mjɔ̰³¹ 'how many'
      INTERROG   many   diachronic syllable
      PREFIX   reduction

Zaiwa verbal particles and adverbials are also weak with respect to stress. This predisposes them to initial consonant elision and tonal assimilation as discussed in §6.7.

---

[74]Burling (1967:23) states that "Maru weak or toneless syllables" occasionally "alternate with syllables having full tone, and it would seem that under certain unknown conditions, full syllables may be reduced to toneless ones."

[75]There is one interesting restriction in the vowel reduction process. The vowel [ə] never follows /ŋ j ɹ h/. In word-initial, open syllables, [a] only follows /ŋ j ɹ h l/ and /ʔ/. Motivation for this restriction is not clearly seen. The only overlap between C_is of unstressed and stressed initial CV syllables is /l ʔ/. Therefore, it would be possible to say that [ə] is in complementary distribution with [a] in the nonoverlapping environments.

/a/→ [ə] / #$C_{1\_}.S_2$ C_1 = all Cs except /ŋ j ɹ h/ S_2 = C(C)V(C) [presyllable]
[a] / #$C_{3\_}.S_2$ C_3 = /ŋ j ɹ h l ʔ/

[76]Both of these processes are common in Tibeto-Burman languages.

Aspects of Zaiwa Segmental Phonology

Zaiwa also has a few reduced syllables occurring word internally, but never word finally. Like typical reduced syllables, the word-internal reduced syllables are open and have a reduced vowel. These syllables correspond with the alternating light-heavy rhythm pattern already discussed, with the rhythm group beginning at the right end of the root as shown in (89).

(89) [mjɔʔ³².ə².dʒɪt³².ɛ²]   'blind'   [ga⁵².ʔə².gɔ⁴³]   'said'
       h l h   h l h

5.3 Zaiwa consonants

In this section, Zaiwa consonants will be discussed at the phonetic and phonemic levels. The phonological processes involving prosodic features affecting Zaiwa consonants will also be presented.

5.3.1 Phonemic representation of consonants

The chart of Zaiwa consonant phonemes is shown in (90).

(90)

		Labial	Alveolar	Alveo-palatal	Palatal	Velar	Glottal
Plosive	vl asp	pʰ	tʰ			kʰ	ʔ
	vd	b [p]	d [t]			g [k]	
Affricate	vl asp		tsʰ	tʃʰ			
	vd		dz [ts]	dʒ [tʃ]			
Fricative	vl		s	ʃ			h
Nasal		m	n			ŋ	
Lateral			l				
Approx		w [v, βʷ]	ɹ		j		

In the chart, the allophonic variants of phonemic consonants are shown in brackets. The consonant phonemes correspond almost perfectly with those suggested by Bradley for Proto-Tibeto-Burman (1979:117).[77] The only differences are an absence of an /x/ and a /z/ in Zaiwa. It is likely that the /x/ and /h/ have merged in Zaiwa and that the /z/ and

---

[77]Matisoff (1973a:2) posits four Proto-Tibeto-Burman series of stops: plain, preglottalized, aspirated, and prenasalized. He states that in Lahu the plain and preglottalized merged into a plain set of stops, the aspirated retained their features, and the prenasalized stops formed a voiced series. This agrees with the two phonemic series and the allophonic variant series shown in (90).

/dz/ have merged. In fact some of the /h/ phonemes tend to have friction and some of the /dz/ phonemes tend to have minimal affrication, but no contrastive pairs have been found to differentiate them. Consonantal contrasts are recorded in appendix A, §A.1.

All affricates presented in (90) are interpreted as single segments. The glides [j] and [w] are treated as consonants syllable initially. The glide [j] is treated as a consonant following C_1 in a consonant cluster, including the [nj] cluster, which is often interpreted as a single segment in other Tibeto-Burman languages.[78] The [j] and [w] following a vowel in the same syllable are interpreted as their vocalic counterparts, [i] and [u], as the second member of a diphthong. Voiced and voiceless plosives deserve comment here. There are voiced plosives in modal syllables[79] which seem to be strongly voiced (45 ms average voicing by five CECIL measurements) and others which are weakly voiced (28 ms average voicing by ten CECIL measurements) with no apparent conditioning factors.[80] The difference is likely due to their historical origins. Matisoff (1978:47) comments on this process; "In many cases the [+voice] versus [−voice] phenomenon can clearly be demonstrated to be due to the effect of the prefixes on the C_i. For example, the old nasal prefix *N- typically voiced a following surd C_i."[81] He also cautions that the reasons involved sometimes remain obscure. The unaspirated, voiceless affricates, [ts] and [tʃ], are rare and are very close to their voiced counterparts. The [h] has a slightly fricative quality at times and may be an [x] with light velar friction.

5.3.2 Deaspiration or devoicing of plosives and affricates

The phonetic voiceless unaspirated plosive series may be analyzed in several different ways. They tend to only appear in tense syllables. Burling (1967:16) included the voiceless unaspirated plosive series in his phonemic inventory as a glottalized plosive series due to diachronic considerations from a reconstructed glottalized plosive series in Tibeto-Burman. However, this solution would require that we posit another phonemic series of preglottalized affricates, nasals, liquids, and glides in order to be consistent in analysis with a glottalized series to derive tense voice.

It is simpler and more efficient to present the voiceless unaspirated plosive series as allophones of another plosive series. This, in essence, is what Yabu (1988) has done. There are two allophonic alternations which

---

[78][nj] behaves identically to all other Nj clusters.
[79]The effect of tense voice quality on the initial consonant will be discussed in §5.3.3.
[80]Voiceless plosives which are found in tense syllables average 9 ms low energy perturbation according to CECIL calculations.
[81]In this case [+voice] and [−voice] correspond to strongly voiced versus weakly voiced, respectively. Surd is another name for voiceless.

Aspects of Zaiwa Segmental Phonology

are possible to explain the presence of the voiceless unaspirated plosive series. Voiced plosives and voiceless aspirated plosives both appear in modal syllables while voiceless unaspirated plosives do not. Therefore, voiceless unaspirated plosives could be in complementary distribution with the voiced plosives or the voiceless aspirated plosives in tense syllables. It is not readily apparent which process takes place or if there is neutralization of contrast between voiced and voiceless aspirated plosives syllable initially in tense syllables. Both analyses seem plausible and will be discussed here.

A voiced plosive initiating a tense syllable would tend towards voicelessness due to tension on the vocal folds. A greater degree of subglottal pressure is necessary to vibrate the tense vocal folds, but the increased airflow is not available due to the closed oral cavity. The laryngeal node of the plosive is associated with the [+stiff vf] autosegment, which indicates redundant voicelessness in obstruents as shown in the redundancy rule (57) in §4.4.3. Note the example for [pɔʔ³¹] 'frog' shown in (91).

(91)

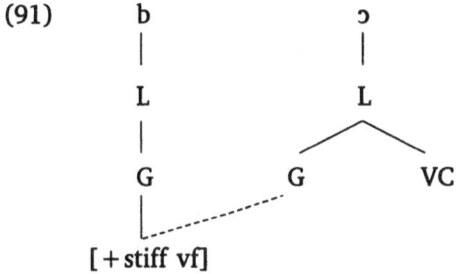

Another piece of evidence for devoicing comes from the causative morpheme [+stiff vf]. Tibeto-Burman languages sometimes use features of the glottis as suprasegmental morphemes to mark causation or transitivity derived from simplex verbs. This process has been traced by Matisoff (1975:151) to a historical Proto-Yi-Burmese *(ʔ) prefix or an alternative exploitation of creaky tone in Burmese. Zaiwa can increase transitivity by applying tense voice to words.[82] For example, [njɛ³.ɛ³] 'hot' versus [njɛ̰⁵³.ɛ³²] 'to burn' and [nun⁴.ɛ⁴] 'shake^intransitive' versus [nṵn⁵³.ɛ³] 'to shake^transitive'. Tense voice also devoices the initial consonant as shown in the pairs, [dzɔ³¹] 'eat' versus [tsɔ³¹] 'make eat' and [bup³] 'rotten' versus [pṵp⁵] 'make rot'.[83] No examples of voiceless, aspirated initial plosives varying with voiceless, unaspirated initial plosives in causative pairs have been found to date.

There is also some support for a voiceless aspirated stop alternation with voiceless unaspirated stops. An aspirated/unaspirated correlation with

---

[82]In some words, tone also changes when a causative autosegment is associated. This will be discussed in §6.3.2.

[83]The tense examples from these two pairs came from Xu and Xu (1984).

modal and tense voice, respectively, is parallel to Lewis' (1968:9) interpretation of Akha; "The quality of the following 9 consonants is determined by the quality of the following vowel. The consonant is aspirated when followed by an oral vowel, and unaspirated when followed by a laryngealized vowel." Hanson (1982:76) describes the same process for Akha and Hani: "In both Akha and Hani initial voiceless consonants are always aspirated in non-laryngealized syllables, and non-aspirated in laryngealized ones." Deaspiration is a likely result phonetically since aspiration, which has the feature [+spread vf], and tense voice, which has the features [+const vf] and [+stiff vf], require a different state of the glottis, while tense voice and voicing can and do co-occur in Zaiwa in tense syllables with syllable-initial voiced affricates, glides, laterals, and nasals. Complementary distribution between the voiceless unaspirated plosive series in tense syllables, and both the voiced plosive series and voiceless aspirated plosive series can be seen in (92).

(92)   [kɔ̰⁵³.ɛ³¹]   [kʰɔ⁵³.ɛ³¹]   [gɔ³.ɛ³]
       'big'   'bitter'   'dance'

       [taḭ⁵³.ɛ²]   [tʰai⁵⁴.lum⁵³.ɛ¹²]
       'tell'   'exchange'

       [taṵ³¹.ɛ¹²]   [tʰau⁵⁴.ɛ²¹]   [dau³.bi⁵³.ɛ²¹]
       'answer'   'stab'   'return an item'

The deaspiration of a plosive, however, is not supported by the feature geometry proposed for Zaiwa in §4.4.1. The glottal node of an aspirated consonant is underlyingly [+spread vf] and, therefore, association of the glottal node with the [+stiff vf] autosegment for tense voice would not be possible. The absence of intransitive/transitive pairs marked by tense voice in words with initial aspirated C_is also argues against deaspiration as a process. Analysis of the affricate series, however, gives some weak evidence that both devoicing and deaspiration may be occurring. The affricates [ts] and [tʃ] both occur in tense syllables. There is only one example of an unaspirated alveolar affricate as the initial consonant of a tense syllable, [tsṵŋ⁵³.ɛ] 'same', which is not enough for discussion.[84] But there are sufficient examples of both [tʃ] and [dʒ] as initial consonants in tense syllables. Noting the existence of voiced affricates in tense syllables, such as [dʒap̰⁵⁴.e³] 'narrow', it would be possible to analyze the initial consonant of [tʃṵ⁵p.e³²] 'suck' as an allophone of /tʃʰ/ and not /dʒ/. However, the voicing

---

[84]Xu and Xu (1984) give the example [dzɔ³¹] 'eat' versus [tsɔ̰³¹] 'make eat', as a non-causative/causative pair, which shows that [ts] is a devoiced allophone of /dz/ in tense syllables.

distinction between [dʒ] and [tʃ] in tense syllables is difficult to hear, and may simply be a limitation of the researcher. The analysis of tense voice in affricates does not give any conclusive evidence for or against the process of deaspiration. Devoicing seems to be the process acting on voiced affricates in tense syllables in the same way it occurs with voiced plosives.

The reason that the alveopalatal affricate initial /dʒ/ shows variation between voiced [dʒ] and voiceless unaspirated [tʃ] in tense syllables may be due to the transitional state of the affrication between an affricate and a [dj] cluster. While plosives are devoiced when associated with a [+stiff vf] autosegment, sonorants are not. Therefore, an affricate, which could be interpreted as a plosive plus a palatal glide, may retain some voicing properties since voicing is not redundant with the glottal features of sonorants. This is shown graphically in (93).

(93)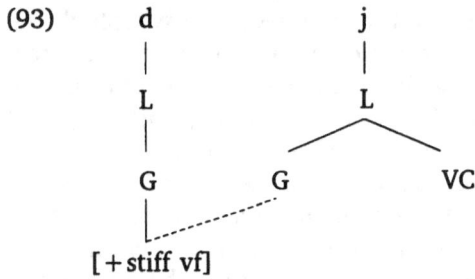

The transitional or intermediate nature of the alveopalatal affricates between affricates and Cj clusters is shown by effects on syllable structure parallel to Cj clusters as shown in §5.2.3, and gaps in distribution as shown in appendix A, §A.5. The ambiguity is reinforced by the nature of affricate voicing in tense syllables, which can parallel the voicing expected for Cj clusters. The devoicing which does occur shows that the [j] portion of the affricate may be in the process of losing its voicing node and merging with the preceding plosive.

The analysis of the voiceless unaspirated plosive series as allophones of the voiced plosive series is indicated by the preceding discussion. Further investigation needs to be done beginning with searching for causative/non-causative verb pairs with aspirated plosive initials. Additional phonological processes affecting consonants are found in appendix A, §A.2.

5.4 Zaiwa vowels

In this section, Zaiwa vowels will be discussed at the phonetic and phonemic levels. Vowel shortening will also be presented.

5.4.1 Phonemic representation of vowels

The chart of Zaiwa simple vowel phonemes is shown in (94).

(94)

	Front unround	Mid unround	Back round
High	i [ɪ]		u [ʊ, ɨ, ɯ]
Mid	e [ɛ, æ]		
Low		a [ə]	ɔ

In (94) the allophonic variants of phonemic vowels are shown in brackets. The vowels [æ ɨ ɯ] are very rare, occurring less than 1% of the time. All vowels except [æ ə ɯ] occur in tense syllables.

The only possible sequences of vowels and glides in the syllable rhyme of CVC or CCVC syllables in the phonetic data are [aj], [aw], and rarely [ɔj]. This limitation in distribution leads to the interpretation of the possible VC rhymes [aj], [aw], and [ɔj], as the diphthongs [ai], [au], and [ɔi], respectively. The only occurrence of [w] as the second member of a consonant cluster is observed in the sequence Cwi. This limitation in occurrence suggests that [wi] following a syllable-initial consonant is the diphthong [ui]. The combination [wi] can still occur syllable initially. The diphthongs [ui] and [ɔi] are generally longer than the other diphthongs and at times appear to be almost bisyllabic as discussed in §5.2.3. The Zaiwa diphthong phonemes are shown in (95). The four diphthongs maximize oral space and vowel distance.

(95)　　/au ai ui ɔi/

All vowels and diphthongs can carry tense voice.
Vocalic contrasts are recorded in appendix A, §A.3.

5.4.2 Vowel shortening

Vowel length in an open syllable is reduced when the syllable is followed by the initial consonant of a following syllable word internally. This process reduces a long vowel to a single mora, reducing tone length as shown in §6.3.1, without destressing the syllable, which is shown by the retention of contrastive tone. Note the examples in (96).

(96)　　/ʃɔ^{31}/ [ʃɔ^{31}] 'meat, flesh'　　/ʃɔ^{31}.k^{h}at.e^4/ [ʃɔ^3.k^{h}at^{54}.e^{21}] 'hunt'

This process is represented in the rule in (97).

Aspects of Zaiwa Segmental Phonology 85

(97)   V: → V / _ $C

The counterprocess of vowel lengthening is not indicated due to the fact that contrast between mid falling tone and high-mid level tone would be neutralized in their citation forms. Since tone contrast is only indicated in isolation, the process of shortening is more phonologically plausible. Further phonological processes affecting vowels are recorded in appendix A, §A.4.

5.5 Distribution of phonemes, tonemes, and voice quality

In this section a brief overview of the distribution of phonemes, tonemes, and voice quality will be given. Additional information concerning distribution is recorded in appendix A, §A.5.

All Zaiwa consonants can appear syllable initially. Syllable finally, the inventory is limited to voiceless plosives (i.e., allophones of voiced plosives) and nasals. The initial consonant in a consonant cluster (C_1) is a stop or nasal and the second member (C_2) is generally /j/ and occasionally /ɹ/.[85] The consonant clusters as onset combinations shown in the table in (98) have been observed.

(98)   /j/   /ɹ/

/pʰ/	x	
/b/	x	
/tʰ/		
/d/		
/kʰ/	x	x
/g/	x	x
/m/	x	
/n/	x	
/ŋ/		

As C_2, /j/ only follows noncoronal plosives and [−high] nasals. The absence of the coronal plosives /tʰ/ and /d/ preceding /j/, and the existence of the alveopalatal affricates /tʃʰ/ and /ʤ/, calls for a possible reinterpretation of /tʃʰ/ and /ʤ/ as /tʰj/ and /dj/, respectively. Evidence for the affricate interpretation comes from the different status of Cj clusters in vowel rules when compared to alveopalatal affricates as shown in appendix A, (184) and (192), and from native speaker intuition which interprets the

---

[85] /ɹ/ tends to only occur in words borrowed from Jinghpaw.

alveopalatal affricates as a single unit. Evidence for the Cj interpretation comes from the gap in the CC clusters as already mentioned and from the parallel occurrence of vowel restrictions following /Cj/ and alveopalatal affricates as shown in (213) appendix A. The merger of plosives and /j/ to form affricates is a live process in Tibeto-Burman (Hongkai 1986:8–9, 17) and may be at an intermediate stage in Zaiwa, allowing both features of Cj clusters and affricates to be interpreted as single units. It may be that Zaiwa is approaching the end of a diachronic process in which a Cj cluster becomes an alveopalatal affricate. In this case, a rule fusing the /Cj/ → [alveopalatal affricate] would be needed early in the phonology. However, native speaker intuition will be given the most weight in this analysis, and affricates will continue to be interpreted as single units synchronically.

As C_2, /ɿ/ follows only [+high] plosives. This is due to common occurrence of these consonant clusters in words borrowed from Jinghpaw.

Tense vowels do not occur following aspirated obstruents and voiceless fricatives, all of which have the feature [+spread vf]. According to Burling (1967), the lack of tense vowels following voiceless fricatives is due to the lack of these consonants in a historical preglottalized series in Tibeto-Burman. However it is interpreted, the phonetic motivation seems obvious as a [+spread vf] segment is incompatible with a [+const vf] autosegment.

All vowels can occur as the nucleus of open syllables. All monophthongs can occur in closed syllables. Diphthongs occur only in open syllables.

All modal and tense vowels occur with all phonemic tones.[86]

All phonemic tones occur with all unchecked syllable types. For tone in checked syllables see §6.4.

Tense voice occurs with all vowel phonemes and in both open and closed syllables, but is absent on unstressed reduced syllables.

Allophonic statements and a discussion of morphophonemic processes are found in appendix A, §§A.6 and A.7, respectively.

---

[86]Tense /e/ does not occur with tone 4 in this data, most likely due to lack of tense /e/.

6
Zaiwa Suprasegmental Phonology

6.1 Introduction to Zaiwa tone

Zaiwa has three contrastive tones:
  53 high falling
  4 high-mid level
  31 mid falling

The phonetic realization of the phonemic tones is indicated below without reference to variations due to allotonic variation. The three aforementioned phonemic tones only occur in unchecked syllables.

Phonetic realization of 53. The high falling tone is generally realized phonetically as a 53. It can be shortened in an open syllable by a plosive or affricate initial of a following syllable word internally (5, 54) or can fall further when in an open or unchecked syllable word finally (52, 51).

Phonetic realization of 4. The high-mid level tone is generally realized phonetically between a 3 and 4 level tone (3, 4, 34, 43).

Phonetic realization of 31. The mid falling tone is generally realized phonetically as a 31. It can be shortened in an open syllable by a plosive or affricate initial of a following syllable word internally (3, 32).

The chart in (99) displays superimposed CECIL plots of each tone to show their relationships in the tonal space.

(99)   CECIL traces of tone 53 [ŋam⁵³.ɛ³¹] 'delicious' (dashed line), tone 4 [ŋam³.ɛ³] 'cold object' (dotted line), and tone 31 [ŋam³¹.ɛ¹²] 'salty' (solid line).[87]

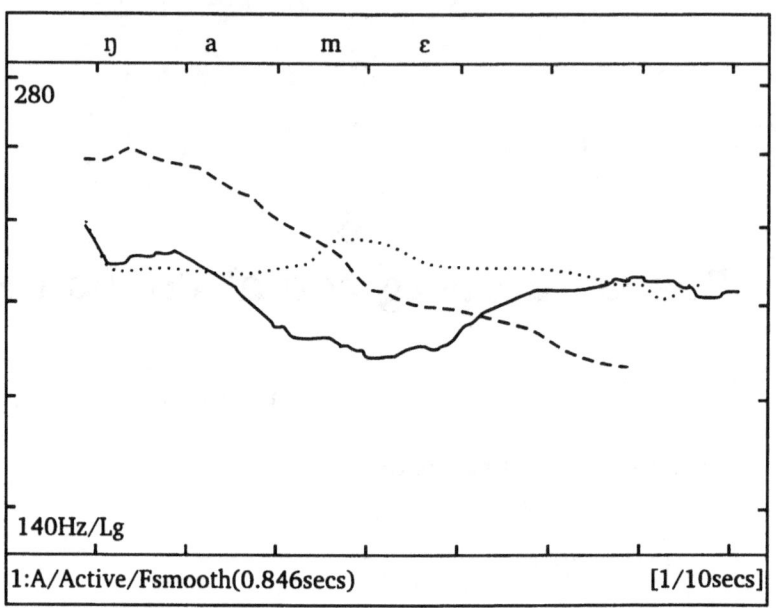

Zaiwa also has pitch variants in checked syllables that are predictable from the glottal features of C_i and voice quality. Since the tone is predictable, no lexical tone assignment is required. Tone in checked syllables was introduced in §§4.1.3 and 4.4 and will be discussed further in §6.4.

A low tone may also exist and is generally phonetically realized at a level 2 or variant thereof (2, 23, 1, 21). Further comment will be made on the questionable existence of a low tone in §6.6.

Sonorant moras (vowels and nasals in the rhyme) carry contrastive pitch. Some borrowed Jinghpaw words have syllabic nasals which carry tone assimilating to the following tone, e.g., [ŋ⁴⁵.gɔ⁵³.gɔk⁴] 'scorpion'.

Each tone can occur with any rhyme and with tense or modal voice quality.

Zaiwa tone undergoes allotonic and tone sandhi processes, and stress/tone interactions that will be discussed in §§6.3 and 6.7.

---

[87]The position of the phonetic characters at the top of the chart approximate the onset of corresponding sounds for each tone plot. A single tone number in the phonetic transcription of tone, e.g., 3 in [ŋam³.ɛ³] 'cold object', simply indicates level pitch and is not an indicator of a short tone duration. The duration of tone is determined by the length of the rhyme as discussed in §6.3.1.

6.2 Tone in reduced syllables

Reduced syllables do not carry contrastive tone in many Tibeto-Burman languages. Morse comments on this phenomenon,

> Languages which exhibit peripheral "affixed" syllables also tend to exhibit within the tonal system one non-contrastive or neutral tone, such as occurs in Rawang. This is especially common among the Tibeto-Burmic languages, which tend to exhibit the occurrence of an initial neutral tone syllable, which may sound like any of the other tones (depending on the environment), but is defined by its lack of significant contrast. (1962:70)

Benedict (1948:1) notes that Southeast Asian languages may have a "marked reduction in possibilities of tonal contrast in unstressed (zero stress) syllables." This reduced syllable never stands alone and is never the final syllable in a root. Tibeto-Burman languages which have reduced syllables and/or unstressed suffixes (Rawang, Maru, Ngochang/Achang, Burmese, Manipuri, etc.) tend not to assign these peripheral syllables any tone, but instead, the actual phonetic tone is determined by the following tone for prefixes and the preceding tone for suffixes (Morse 1988:130). Yip (1995:493), commenting on Chinese, states that "it is entirely possible that many syllables may leave the phonology still toneless, and have their pitch filled in by the phonetic component."

Nonproductive, reduced syllables in Zaiwa do not carry tone in the same sense as other syllables. Nonproductive, reduced syllables seem to assimilate to the following tone and are thus noncontrastive. Assimilation occurs only if the consonant following the reduced vowel is a sonorant. If the following consonant is a sonorant, the tone of the following syllable spreads to the reduced syllable. The mechanism of spread may proceed as follows. The reduced vowel of the reduced syllable does not have its own voice node. This phenomenon can be seen when a reduced vowel is voiceless when preceded and followed by voiceless obstruents, e.g., [tʃʰə̥8.tʃʰi53] /tʃʰətʃʰi53/ 'deer'. The reduced vowel is voiced and carries pitch, however, if the following consonant is voiced, e.g., [tsʰə54.wam53] from /tsʰəwam53/ 'wall'. I analyze such occurrences as a result of the voice node of the following consonant spreading to the reduced vowel. Since pitch is a dependent feature of the voice node, the pitch on a voiced sonorant is included in the spread of voice. The pitch of the vowel in the full syllable spreads to the empty voice node of the preceding sonorant consonant, which, not being moraic, does not manifest contrastive tone, but still may have associated pitch.[88] The vowel in the reduced

---

[88] Pitch manifest on a nonmoraic sonorant is demonstrated in word-initial sonorants where pitch rises from a neutral 3 position to a 5 preceding a 53 tone as shown in (30).

syllable has an empty laryngeal node and is open for spreading of the feature voice from the following sonorant as shown in (100).

(100) [tsʰə⁵⁴.wam⁵³] 'wall'

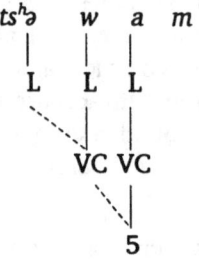

The voice node can spread across syllable boundaries, whereas the glottal node spread is restricted to segments of the same syllable. If the C following the reduced vowel is an obstruent, there is no voice node and spreading cannot occur. In this case, the reduced vowel receives its voicing from the initial consonant of the reduced syllable according to the rules shown in (56) and (57). These processes are summarized in (63). The pitch on the reduced vowel of 'child' (101) is derived by a default rule, inasmuch as voiced segments must have pitch.

(101) [tʃʰə̣.tʃʰi⁵³] 'deer'   [dʒə³.ʃaŋ⁵³] 'child'

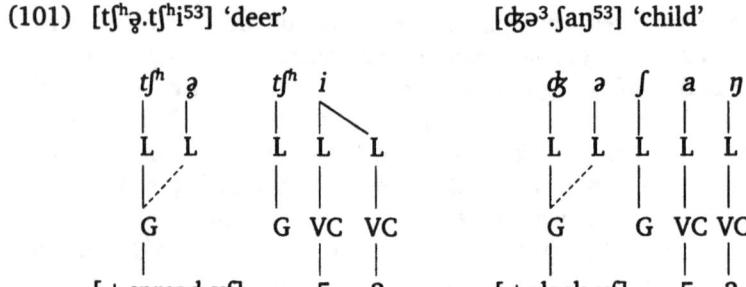

Note the additional examples in (102).

(102) [lə³.mjuʔ³²]   /ləmjuʔ³¹/   'monkey'
      [bə¹.mau¹]   /bəmau²/   'beard'
      [lə³.dʒaŋ⁵³.e³¹] /lədʒaŋ⁵³e⁴/ 'prepare'

Productive reduced syllables and normal syllables reduced by nonstressed speech carry the contrastive tone of their nonreduced forms, e.g., [ʃɔ³¹] /ʃɔ³¹/ 'flesh' versus [ʃə³¹.mjɛn⁵¹] /ʃɔ³¹mjen⁵³/ 'fat'.[89]

The examples discussed in this section show that tone in nonproductive, reduced syllables behaves differently than tone in fully stressed syllables. Historical epenthesis of the reduced vowels may be responsible for the differing feature geometry of the reduced vowels.

6.3 Tonal processes in close juncture

In this section the focus is on the influence of tones on neighboring tones in a sequence, or TONE SANDHI. Only the tone sandhi phenomena relevant to Zaiwa tonal changes will be discussed here. Tone sandhi is defined by Ladefoged (1993:256) as "changes in tone due to the influence of one tone on another." But in Asian languages this definition is not completely accurate. Asian languages tend to also have tone sandhi conditioned by positional factors. Therefore, the definition must be expanded for Asian languages to include the influence of structural positions and intonation (Laver 1994:474). Tone sandhi may be phonologically conditioned as in assimilation, grammatically conditioned based on grammatical function changes, or occur dependent on positional factors in which adjacent syllables cause tone changes which cannot be explained by either assimilation or grammatical conditioning. Each of these three processes will be discussed separately.

6.3.1 Allotonic tonal processes

Shortening. Tone length is generally dictated by syllable length. The shorter the duration of the syllable, the less time the tone has to fall. CECIL measurements confirm that a vowel in a checked syllable, or in an open syllable followed by a plosive or affricate, is one timing unit long (measured as ~100 ms for comparative purposes), while a vowel in an open syllable or a VN rhyme is at least two timing units long (~200 ms).[90] For example, the chart in (103) is the CECIL tone plot for [ʃɪ³.pʰjik⁵.neᶜ⁵³.ʃi³¹] 'red pepper' shows the same morpheme, [ʃi³¹] 'fruit', occurring word initially and word finally. Word initially, however, the rhyme is only one mora long and word finally it is more than two moras long.

---

[89]Weidert (1979:89) suggests that a related language, Jinghpaw, has two tones, a high and a low, in prefix-type syllables with a schwa as vowel, although no contrastive pairs were shown.

[90]A sampling of CECIL calculations showed that checked syllables average .11 seconds, open syllables average .22 seconds, and syllables closed by a nasal average .24 seconds in duration.

(103) CECIL tone plot for [ʃɪ³.pʰjik⁵.neᵋ⁵³.ʃi³¹] /ʃi³¹pʰjikne⁵³ʃi³¹/ 'red pepper'

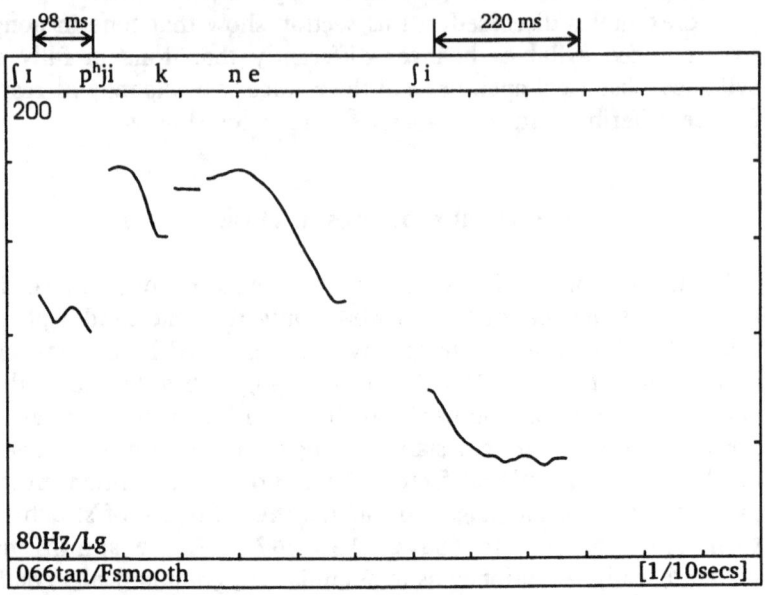

Open or nasal final syllables followed by nonplosive, nonaffricate initials of the following syllable tend to be shorter than open or nasal-final syllables word finally, but longer than a single mora.

High falling tone (53) is thus shortened to high, level, and short (5), or high, partially falling (54), in open syllables followed by a plosive or affricate as the initial consonant of the following syllable. Note the examples shown in (104).

(104) [ha⁵⁴.tʃʰɪ³².tʃʰi⁵².ε²¹]   /ha⁵³tʃʰi³¹tʃʰi⁵³e⁴/   'sneeze'
       [ʔə³.tʃʰa⁵.ʔə³.ʤʊt⁴.mu³¹.ε¹]   /atʃʰa⁵³a³ʤʊtmu³¹e⁴/   'dirty'

This leads to the rule shown in (105).[91]

(105) 53 → 5, 54 / _ $ $\begin{bmatrix} -\text{cont} \\ -\text{son} \end{bmatrix}$

---

[91]The use of two possible outputs for a tone in a particular environment, e.g., 5, 54, represents the continuum within which the pitch varies. This may blur the distinction between category oriented phonology and continuum oriented phonetics, but it does represent the complexity of the situation more adequately.

The shortening process can be represented autosegmentally by associating the first tone of a contour tone to the nuclear vowel and stranding the second tone with no mora to associate with, which then gets stray erased as shown in (106).

(106)

$$\begin{matrix} & & & \begin{bmatrix} -\text{cont} \\ -\text{son} \end{bmatrix} \\ C & V & \$ & C \\ & | & & \\ & 5\ \ 3 & & \\ & \ \ \searrow & & \end{matrix}$$

Mid falling tone (31) is shortened to mid, level, and short (3), or mid slightly falling (32), in open syllables with an obstruent as C_i of the following syllable. The motivation for this sort of tone leveling could be both that checked syllables are shorter and that a following tone is found at the same level or higher level as in the assimilation discussed in §6.3.2. For nonfinal syllables it is unclear which motivation is more active. My assumption here is that in nonfinal syllables, both are active. Note the examples shown in (107).

(107) [mau³².kʰuŋ⁵³]   /mau³¹kʰuŋ⁵³/   'sky'
      [daŋ³².bau³]   /daŋ³¹bau⁴/   'thigh'

This leads to the rule shown in (108).

(108)   31 → 3, 32 / _ $ $\begin{bmatrix} -\text{cont} \\ -\text{son} \end{bmatrix}$

Rules (105) and (108) may be generalized as shown in (109).

(109)   falling tone → level tone / _ $ $\begin{bmatrix} -\text{cont} \\ -\text{son} \end{bmatrix}$

In checked syllables, a single checked tone is posited with allotonic variants conditioned by the glottal features of the initial consonant and voice quality. This tone does, however, differ in degree of allowed fall depending on the final stops. The final stops [pʔ tʔ kʔ] tend to allow partial to no fall except when utterance final, while a final [ʔ] allows a partial to full fall as the final stressed syllable in a word, and a partial fall when word internal. The degree of pitch drop with each final stop in Zaiwa is shown in (110) with examples in (111).

(110) Final stop   Word final   Word internal
     -p^{92} -t -k   5, 54   5
                       3, 32   3
      -ʔ   54, 53   5, 54
                      32, 31   3, 32

(111) [dau³.kɔp³¹]   'turtle'   [lə³.kʰap³²]   'trousers'
      [kʰjup⁵⁴.e²¹]   'sew'
      [pjḙt⁴]   'duck'
      [pʰat⁵.e²]   'vomit'   [mɪt³.ɛ³]   'think'
      [ʔə³.sɪk⁵⁴]   'new'   [sɪk⁵.ʃi³¹]   'fruit'
      [mjṵʔ³¹]   'this place'
      [banᵋ.ʃɔʔ⁵³]   'all'   [ʔa³.tʰɔʔ⁵⁴]   'blunt'
      [tʰɔʔ⁵⁴.ɛ³²]   'sharp'   [kʰjuʔ⁵³.juʔ³¹]   'six persons'
      [mjuʔ³.nɔʔ³²]   'gibbon'

The motivation for falling pitch and the differences between the co-articulated oral/glottal stops and the glottal stop were briefly discussed in §3.4.3 and will be expanded upon here. To review briefly, the vowel portion of a syllable checked by a glottal stop is allowed to bleed into the glottal stop up to the point of complete glottal closure or cessation of vocal fold vibration, effectively lengthening the vowel. Therefore the tone drop is longer. This is generally supported by CECIL pitch and vowel length measurements as well. In these syllables the glottal closure is simply the end of the vowel which is 1.5–2 moras long.⁹³ This fall is shortened by the oral portion of final [pʔ tʔ kʔ], which gives the shorter pitch fall observed in these syllables. The extent of fall word finally in contrast to less fall word internally is due to a domain final effect, which allows more of a drop word finally. One further observation is that /Cj/ clusters in stopped syllables can increase the length of the fall due to the pitch carrying ability of the /j/.

The mechanism by which pitch is induced to fall in checked syllables has been discussed in the literature. The process occurs in Lahu and is described by Matisoff (1973a:25); "the quick drop in energy caused by the abrupt glottal closure conveys the impression of a fall in pitch." Whether the pitch in Lahu actually drops or simply gives the impression of a drop is not clear.

---

⁹²It is interesting to note that in Zaiwa, a syllable-final [pʔ] may allow partial to full pitch fall word finally, very similar to a glottal stop. The reason for this is most likely due to the size of the oral cavity. A labial stop gives the maximal oral cavity (including the buccal cavity) of any stop. There is sufficient oral volume for the lungs to push air past the glottis, allowing a partial to total fall in pitch. A partial fall in pitch is observed with final [tʔ] and [kʔ], but almost never a complete fall.

⁹³It could be argued that a mora cannot be quantified with fractions of a unit, but in this case stretching the phonological definition helps to envision the lengthening process.

Zaiwa Suprasegmental Phonology

In Zaiwa, however, the pitch does actually drop as can be seen in the previous CECIL tone plots.

A syllable-final co-articulated oral/glottal stop occludes the airflow completely and quickly and allows little or no air to pass by the glottis, greatly reducing the drop in pitch. On the other hand, a syllable-final incomplete glottal stop, which occurs in Zaiwa, is not as abrupt and allows for some air to leak past the glottis, sustaining audible phonation and giving a partial to full pitch drop. The partial to full drop allowed by the incomplete glottal stop can be looked at as an intermediate "creaky" phonation stage on its way to total occlusion or cessation of phonation. Creaky phonation corresponds with a drop in pitch. The timing implicit in this process is shown graphically in the chart in (112).

(112) Oral and glottal closures versus time

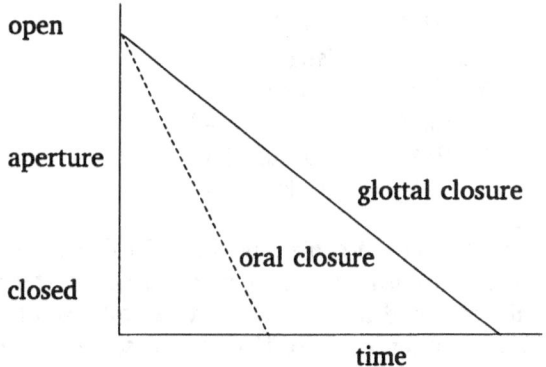

The falling effect motivated by final stops would seem to argue for a single tone in checked syllables instead of variants of the high falling and mid falling tones. The tone height is derived from the laryngeal features of the surrounding consonants and voice quality, as discussed in §4.4, and the falling contour is a product of glottal closure. Zee and Maddieson (1979) express a similar interpretation for the Shanghai dialect of Chinese in proposing that the sharp fall in syllables closed by a glottal stop is caused by the closing action of the vocal cords to a glottal stop, and, therefore, the fall is not included in the underlying tone since it is predictable.

Limited fall conditioned by rhyme and following particle.[94] Mid falling tone (31) tends to become mid, slightly falling (32) when associated with a verb or adjective with a glide/vowel series, or a rhyme

---

[94]In a strict sense, this rule is based both on allotonic and tone sandhi processes as the terms are used in this study. The process is placed under the allotonic section for convenience only.

consisting of a diphthong or vowel/nasal series, followed by the verbal suffix /e⁴/ (perfective aspect). Verbs and adjectives, which have a simple rhyme or non-nasal final, and nouns with any rhyme and no following suffix do not show this process. The sonorant length of the rhyme seems to be the key factor in preventing the tone from dropping fully and partially assimilating to the height of the following tone on the suffix. The Zaiwa speaker who provided this data was unwilling to produce or accept verbs or adjectives without the aspectual particle attached, so root words in isolation could not be obtained. These observations suggest the rule shown in (113) with the examples in (114).[95]

(113) $31 \rightarrow 32 / \begin{Bmatrix} jV \\ V_d \\ VN \end{Bmatrix} \$e^4$ where V_d = diphthong

(114) [mau³¹]   /mau³¹/   'rain'
       [nɔ³¹.ɛ²]   /nɔ³¹e⁴/   'sick'
       [ŋau³².ɛ²³] /ŋau³¹e⁴/   'weep'
       [lam³².ɛ²]   /la³¹me⁴/   'wide, broad'
       [nji̲³².ɛ²]   /nji̲³¹e⁴/   'located (at)'
       [nɔ³¹.ɛ²]   /nɔ³¹e⁴/   'sick'

This process goes a long way in explaining what Burling (1967:57) describes as a split of Proto-Yi-Burmese tone 2 between nouns and verbs in Zaiwa. Burling describes the mid falling tone on verbs followed by certain suffixes as "mid, even and rather long" (p. 18), and the same tone on nouns as low falling (mid falling in this study).[96] The tonal split based on syntactic class is most likely the allotonic effect described above.

The allotonic processes which act on tone in checked syllables were discussed in §4.4.

6.3.2 Tone sandhi

Zaiwa exhibits three types of tone sandhi: (1) tone sandhi conditioned by assimilation to tones in adjacent syllables, (2) grammatically conditioned tone sandhi, and (3) tone sandhi due to positional phonological variants. The occurrence of each type of tone sandhi in Zaiwa will be discussed in this section.

Tone sandhi conditioned by assimilation to adjacent tones. Assimilation generally proceeds between tone levels. The assimilation of shape or

---

[95]The lowering of tone on the verb-final suffix is discussed in §6.7.
[96]Both my language associate and Burling's were unwilling to say verbs without a suffix attached.

contour is rare. Assimilative tone sandhi is generally retrogressive, i.e., the tone of the following syllable assimilates to the tone of the preceding syllable, or, looking at it another way, the tone of the preceding syllable lasts longer than its own syllable. Assimilative tone sandhi can be either VERTICAL or HORIZONTAL. Vertical assimilation raises or lowers tone in the environment of a higher or lower tone. DOWNDRIFT, L raising before a H (L → M/_H), and FINAL LOWERING[97] are all common examples of vertical assimilation (Hyman 1973:154–56). Horizontal assimilation can be either PARTIAL or COMPLETE. Partial horizontal assimilation results when a tone spreads into a following level tone of different register, creating a contour: L H → L LH. Complete horizontal assimilation results when one register tone or a part of a contour tone is completely absorbed by an adjacent tone: HL L → H L. This process can occur between two noncontour tones as an intermediate stage: L H H → L LH H → L L H. Another common form of horizontal assimilation is the conversion of a HL H to a H 'H, where 'H is a downstepped H.

One additional tonal process closely related to assimilation is SIMPLIFICATION or LEVELING. Tone simplification takes the shapes of individual tones making contour tones and simplifies them into level tones, e.g., HL HL → H HL. Neutralization of different tones into a single tone in certain contexts can also be called simplification, e.g., HM ML → HM ML and HM M → HM ML. Zaiwa exhibits all of the above types of tone sandhi.

Syllable-initial and final consonants can also affect tone sandhi. The main factors in this influence are from voicing and sonority. Vertical assimilations can be affected by the initial consonant of the first syllable of an assimilation or by the intervening consonant(s) between the interacting syllables. In some languages, a syllable with low tone and a voiced obstruent as C_i will not allow the low tone to undergo expected vertical assimilation to a mid tone preceding a high. The voiced obstruent initial blocks the predicted application of the rule. This parallels the correlation between voiced initials and low tone. The same raising process can be blocked when an obstruent is between the two interacting tones, but is allowed when the intervening consonant is [+son]. Hyman (1973:169) comments that in this case the "sonorants ride along the fundamental frequency contour." In some languages, voiced consonants allow horizontal assimilation while voiceless consonants do not (p. 158). In other languages voiced obstruents block spreading of high tone, and voiceless obstruents block the spreading of low tone. The consonants do not motivate the assimilations, they simply block or permit them (1973:166). Zaiwa exhibits tone sandhi rules based on interactions with features of initial and final consonants.

---

[97]A rule by which a final low falls to a rest position.

Leveling conditioned by the following tone. High falling tone becomes high level or high, slightly falling preceding a high falling tone. Note the examples shown in (115) which lead to the rule in (116).

(115) [ju̱m⁵³]   /ju̱m⁵³/   'house'
       [ju̱m⁵⁴.siŋ⁵³.mi³²]   /ju̱m⁵³siŋ⁵³mi³¹/   'female head of house'
       [mə³.ʔʊn⁵³.ʃi³¹]   /maʔun⁵³ʃi³¹/   'coconut'
       [mə³.ʔʊn⁵.gu̱ʔ⁵]   /maʔun⁵³gu̱ʔ/   'coconut shell ladle'
       [mu⁵.lui⁵³.ɛ³¹]   /mu⁵³lui⁵³e⁴/   'and then'

(116) 53 → 5, 54/ ___ 53

Mid falling tone (31) becomes level (3) or slightly falling (32) when it precedes any other tone. The tendencies are for a 31 to become a 3 preceding a 31 when the initial syllable is open and the C_i of the following syllable is a glide or lateral (117a)–(117e); for a 31 to become a 32 preceding a 31 (nondownstepped) when the intervening consonants are obstruents (117f), (117g), (117i); for a 31 to become a 32 preceding a 4 irrespective of the intervening consonants (117j) and (117k); and for a 31 to become a 3 preceding a 53 (117l). Two forces are at work here, namely the leveling ability of the following tone and the shortening ability of the intervening consonants. Each tone and consonant type mentioned seems to have a different assimilative force on the preceding tone. Higher tone and sonorant segments between tones have high assimilative force, which increases leveling. Lower tone and nonsonorant segments between tones disrupt tone spread and have lower assimilative force.

(117) a. [bui³¹]   /bui³¹/   'sunlight'
       b. [bui³.waŋ³¹]   /bui³¹waŋ³¹/   'west'
       c. [bui³.lap⁵⁴.e²¹]   /bui³¹lape⁴/   'to dry'
       d. [dzui³¹]   /dzui³¹/   'teeth'
       e. [dzui³.βʷaŋ³¹]   /dzui³¹waŋ³¹/   'gums'
       f. [bui³².bu³¹]   /bui³¹bu³¹/   'sweat'
       g. [jɔ³².sɔ³¹]   /jɔ³¹sɔ³¹/   'forest'
       h. [mi³¹]   /mi³¹/   'fire'
       i. [mi³².guŋ³¹]   /mi³¹guŋ³¹/   'earth'
       j. [mja̱ŋ³².gum³]   /mja̱ŋ³¹gum⁴/   'shin'
       k. [tʃʰɔ³².hui³]   /tʃʰɔ³¹hui⁴/   'lime for betel'
       l. [mi³.sat⁵⁴.e²¹]   /mi³¹sate⁴/   'extinguish'

The rule, however, may be considered a single rule as shown in (118).

(118) 31 → 3, 32 / ___ 31, 4, 53

This is similar to what Edmondson, et al. (1995) calls the contour smoothing principle which applies in Tibetan and Chinese. The contour smoothing principle states that a high falling tone will change to a high level tone preceding a high tone. This can be generalized to state that a falling tone is leveled preceding a higher tone or a tone at the same height as shown in (119).

(119) X (falling tone) → level / ___ Y (tone higher or equal to X)

Raising conditioned by following tone. High-mid level tone (4) can assimilate to following high tones. In open syllables, tone 4 raises (45, 35) when followed by a 5 if the initial consonant of the following syllable is [+son]. This can be labeled partial horizontal assimilation, a type of tone spread (Hyman 1973:156). Note the examples shown in (120).

(120) [ʔa³.gu³¹]   /ʔa⁴gu³¹/   'younger sibling'
       [ʔa⁴⁵.maŋ⁵³] /ʔa⁴maŋ⁵³/   'elder sibling'
       [ŋa³.nuŋ³]   /ŋa⁴nuŋ⁴/   'we (inclusive)'
       [ŋa³⁵.n̥k⁵]   /ŋa⁴nig̊/   'we (dual)'

If there is an obstruent following the first syllable, the tone in the first syllable stays within normal variations for a (4) tone (e.g., 3, 4, 34, 43), as shown in (121).

(121) [tʰuŋ⁴.tsʰum⁵³] /tʰuŋ⁴tsʰum⁵³/ 'mortar'
       [wɔ⁴.gjɔ⁵³.ɛ²]   /wɔ⁴gjɔ⁵³e/   'hear'
       [tʰuŋ³⁴.gi⁵³]   /tʰuŋ⁴gi⁵³/   'pestle'

This leads to the rule shown in (122).

(122) 4 → 45, 35 / ___C   (C)   V
                    [+son]   [+son] |
                                       5

       3, 4 / ___(C)   C   V
                       ⎡ −cont ⎤ |
                       ⎣ −son ⎦   5

The assimilation depends on the sonorant quality of the consonants between the TBUs. If a sonorant consonant is the only segment between the two TBUs, the segment will act as a bridge between the two tones, raising the tone (4) to a 34 or 45. This process is shown in (123).

(123)

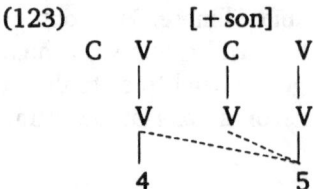

Falling conditioned by preceding tone. High-mid level tone (4) tends to fall (43, 32, 31) following a high falling tone (53) or high, partially falling allotone of a checked syllable. Note the examples shown in (124) which lead to the rule in (125).

(124) [dzə³.mɔ̰³]   /dza⁴mɔ̰⁴/   'father of man's wife'
       [ʔa̰u⁵³.mɔ̰³¹]   /a̰u⁵³mɔ̰⁴/   'mother of man's wife'
       [nji³.gaŋ³.guŋ⁵³]   /nji⁴gaŋ⁴guŋ⁵³/   'noon'
       [nji³⁴.guŋ⁵³.gaŋ³²] /nji⁴guŋ⁵³gaŋ⁴/   'noon (alternate form)'
       [mjɔʔ³².mau³]   /mjɔʔmau⁴/   'eyebrow (eye hair)'
       [ŋ̰ɔʔ⁵⁴.mau³¹]   /ŋ̰ɔʔmau⁴/   'feather (bird hair)'

(125) 4 → 31, 32, 43 / 53, 54 __

The tone change is most likely a phonetic effect of a level tone being caught in the fall of the preceding tone and not a copying of the tonal contour onto the following tone.

Lowering conditioned by preceding tone. High-mid level tone (4) tends to lower to a mid level tone (3) following a preceding phonetic 31 or 32. The preceding fall seems to keep the following level tone at the low end of its phonetic manifestation. Note the examples shown in (126) which lead to the rule in (127).

(126) [ban³².bɔ³]   /ban³¹bɔ⁴/   'flower'
       [mjɔʔ³².mau³]   /mjɔʔmau⁴/   'eyebrow'
       [gɔŋ³².mja̰³]   /gɔŋ³¹mja̰⁴/   'spider'

(127) 4 → 3 / 31, 32 __

It is interesting to note that rules (116) and (127) act simultaneously on the same words in a regular fashion with no 'bleeding' of environments.

Neutralization. There is neutralization of contrast between the high-mid level tone (4) and the mid falling tone (31) in open syllables when followed by another stressed syllable in close juncture. In these environments, both tones can appear phonetically as mid-level tones (3). Neutralization of contrast can also appear between high-mid level tone (4) and mid falling tone (31) following a high falling tone (53) due to the assimilation of high-mid level tone to the preceding falling tone as shown in this §6.3.2. In both cases, phonemic tone can be determined by identifying the morpheme in a nonambiguous environment as shown in (128).

(128) [bjɔ³¹]   /bjɔ³¹/   'bee'
       [bjɔ³.ʃum³¹.mi³.dziŋ⁵³] /bjɔ³¹ʃum³¹mi³¹dziŋ⁵³/   'candle'
       [gaŋ⁴]   /gaŋ⁴/   'middle'
       [nji³.gaŋ³.guŋ⁵³]   /nji³¹gaŋ⁴guŋ⁵³/   'noon'

Downdrift. Downdrift is the lowering of a high tone after a low tone. In this case, the 3 of a 53 can be treated as a phonologically lower tone than the following 5 and downdrift of following 53, either the initial pitch level or entire tone contour can occur. High falling tone can become a high-mid falling (43, 42) or mid falling (31) tone following a high falling tone (53). Note the examples in (129).

(129) [wa̰⁵³]   /wa̰⁵³/   'father'
       [ʔi⁵³.wa̰³¹]   /ʔi⁵³wa̰⁵³/   'father of another'
       [dɔ⁵⁴.dɔ⁴³.ɛ³²]   /dɔ⁵³dɔ⁵³e⁴/   'crawl'

Generally, downdrift does not occur when the consonant immediately following the first tone in the downstep is a nasal (128). The motivation for the exceptions to downdrift in this environment is not clear. These exceptions seem to indicate that downdrift is not a product of loss of airflow, but a process dependent on the features of the consonants between syllable nuclei. More work is needed to determine why downdrift is not active or is blocked in these environments. The examples in (130) lead to the rule in (131).

(130) [jṵm⁵⁴.siŋ⁵³.mi³²]   /jṵm⁵³siŋ⁵³mi⁴/   'female head of house'
       [hu³.sʊn⁵⁴.pʰju⁵¹]   /hu³¹sʊn⁵³pʰju⁵³/   'garlic'
       [tɔ̰⁵⁴.mḭ⁵³.ɛ³²]   /dɔ̰⁵³mḭ⁵³e⁴/   'forget'

This leads to the rule shown in (131).

(131) 53 → 43, 31 / V⁵³ C (C) ___
                    [−nasal]

Downdrift also occurs between words in a phrase (132).

(132) [jų̈m⁵³ mi³¹ jų̈m³¹]   /jų̈m⁵³ mi³¹ jų̈m⁵³/   'four houses (cl)'
      house   four   house^cl

The downdrift for (132) is shown very clearly in the chart in (134).

(133) CECIL tone trace of [jų̈m⁵³ mi³¹ jų̈m³¹] /jų̈m⁵³ mi³¹ jų̈m⁵³/ 'four houses (cl)'.[98]

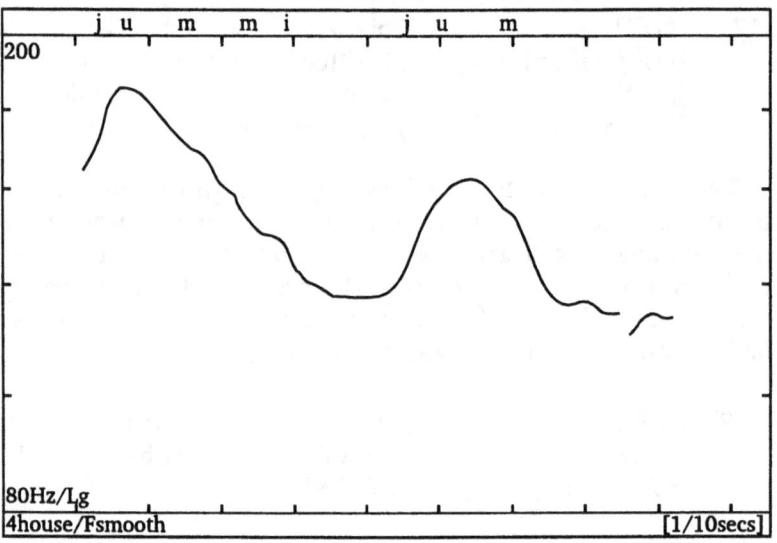

Mid falling tone (31) tends to become a low falling tone (21) following a 31 tone in a syllable closed by a nasal (134), or following a 31 tone in an open syllable with a nasal C_i in the following syllable (133).[99] In this case the 1 of the 31 acts as the low tone to bring the following 31 tone down. The examples in (134) and (135) lead to the rule in (136).

(134) [n̩³.duŋ³².ʃi²¹]   /n̩duŋ³¹ʃi³¹/   'jackfruit'
      [dʒaŋ̩³².gɔn²¹]   /dʒaŋ̩³¹gɔn³¹/   'termite'

---

[98]In this example the morpheme /jų̈m⁵³/ is realized as a high falling tone phrase initially, but, following the 31 tone of /mi³¹/, the high falling tone is lowered to a phonetic 31 tone, [jų̈m³¹].

[99]This is the opposite effect of that shown by an intervening nasal consonant on downdrift of 53 tone as discussed in reference to (131).

(135) [gu³².maŋ²¹]   /gu³¹maŋ³¹/   'brothers and sisters'
      [tsai̯³².mau²¹] /dzai̯³¹mau³¹/   'Kachin state'

(136) 31 → 21 / 31 N (C) ___

The mid-stopped allotone is also lowered by the preceding 31 in the same environment as the nonstopped 31 as seen in (137).

(137) [wɔʔ³.kan³².wɔʔ².e²] /wɔʔkan³¹wɔʔe⁴/ 'weave'
      [dum³².bat².e²]   /dum³¹bade⁴/   'pound (into pulp)'

This leads to the generalization that downstep does occur following a falling tone, but not in identical environments following high falling and mid falling tones.

Grammatically conditioned tone sandhi. Grammatical tone is defined as "the morphological placement of a tone on a particular word or morpheme as the marker of a particular grammatical meaning" (Schuh 1978:252). Grammatically conditioned tone sandhi refers both to tone changes due to the change in part of speech of a word and to tone changes due to a change in the grammatical function of a morpheme. Grammatical tone alternations are common in Tibeto-Burman. Tone change between simplex/causative pairs is well attested (Matisoff 1973a). Bradley (1993:200) notes that it is common for tone to mark a change in pronouns between the subject form and possessor in Yi-Burmese languages. A brief overview is as follows:

1. Tone changes are demonstrated between a verb (53) and a related noun (31, 4) as shown in (138).

(138) [kʰau⁵².ɛ¹]   'steal'   [bju³².kʰau³¹] 'thief (person^steal)'
      [tʰuŋ⁵³.ɛ³²] 'pound (rice)'   [tʰuŋ³⁴.gi⁵³]   'pestle (pounder)'
      [ʃum⁵³.e³²]   'weave rope'   [ʃum³²]   'woven rope'

2. Tone change is demonstrated on a particle marking verb aspect (139): motion toward /lɔ³¹/ versus motion away /lɔ⁴/.

(139) Motion towards speaker   Motion away from speaker

      [lɔ³¹.ɛ¹²]   'come'   [lɔ³.ɛ³²]   'leave'
      [tʰɔt⁵⁴.lɔ³¹.ɛ²]   'come up'   [daŋ⁵³.lɔ³².ɛ²] 'fly away'
      [dum³.lɔ²¹.ɛ¹²]   'return'   [dum³².lɔ³.ɛ³]   'go'

3. Tone change and voice quality change are demonstrated between a transitive verb and a related adjective (140). In these cases a form of causation or transitivity is marked by autosegments. The same process occurs throughout Tibeto-Burman languages. Matisoff (1974:158) states that "there is no simple way of predicting what the tonal variation (if any) will be in any particular simplex/causative pair."[100]

(140) [njɛ̰⁵³.ɛ³²]   'burn (active)'   [njɛ³.ɛ³]   'hot'
      [nṵn⁵³.ɛ³]   'to shake'   [nun⁴.ɛ⁴]   'shake'

4. Tone change is demonstrated depending on location of speaker with reference to the referee (141).

(141) [sum³².juʔ⁴]   'three people (here)'   [sum⁵³.juʔ³¹]   'three people (there)'
      [mi³².juʔ²⁴]   'four people (here)'   [mi⁵³.juʔ³¹]   'four people (there)'

5. Personal pronouns with 31 tone change to 53 tone in the possessive form (142).[101]

(142) [ŋɔ³¹]   'first person singular'   [ŋa⁵³]   'first person singular possessive'
      [naŋ³¹]   'second person singular'   [naŋ⁵³]   'second person' singular possessive'
      [jaŋ̰³¹]   'third person singular'   [jaŋ̰⁵³]   'third person singular possessive'

The tone change cannot be ascribed to the addition of the possessive suffix /e⁴/, as suggested by Xu and Xu (1984) as noted in chapter 2, since the tone change occurs with or without the /e⁴/ suffix.

6. Reduplication. Certain words, generally dealing with bodily function or repetitive actions, use reduplication as an iconic device. The structure of the reduplicated word is generally σ_1. $\sigma_2{}^{31}$. $\sigma_3{}^{53}$. σ_4 with σ_3 a duplication of σ_2, but with a different tone as indicated. σ_3 carries the phonemic tone of the word in isolation, and σ_2 is a lowering of the tone found on σ_3. All examples collected for this paper show σ_3 to be 53 tone (143).

---

[100]The tense voice causativizer raises tone in checked syllables also, but this rise cannot be unambiguously credited to causativization since tense voice raises all tones in checked syllables.

[101]The first-person personal pronoun base form in dual and plural pronouns is /ŋa³¹/. The base form /ŋɔ³¹/ is used for first-person singular. The vowel change from [a] → [ɔ] in first-person singular is idiosyncratic.

(143) [ha⁵⁴.tʃʰɹ³².tʃʰi⁵².ɛ²¹]   'sneeze'
     [mau³.gum³².gum⁵³.e²]   'thunder'   [mau³.gum⁵³.e³²]   'thunder'
     [kʰɹuŋ³.dzau̯³².dzau̯⁵².e²]   'cough'   [dzau̯⁵³.e³²]   'cough'
     [ʔa⁵.ham²¹.ham⁴¹.ɛ¹]   'yawn'
     [guŋ³.tʃʰɹ³.tʃʰi⁵³.ɛ³¹]   'bathe'   [tʃʰi⁵³.ɛ³¹]   'wash'
     [guŋ³².lui³².lui⁵³.ɛ¹]   'swim'

The general pattern for reduplication seems to be a four-syllable elaborate expression. The three-syllable word for 'crawl' manifests the reduplicative tone pattern when the morpheme for 'hand' is added word initially to make a four-syllable word (144).

(144) [lɔʔ³.dɔ³².dɔ⁵¹.ɛ¹]   'crawl'   [dɔ⁵⁴.dɔ⁴³.ɛ²¹]   'crawl'

An exception to this pattern is found in the word 'float,' which is a three-syllable word when reduplicated as shown in (145).

(145) [bjɔm³².bjɔm⁵².ɛ²]   'float'   [bjɔm⁵².ɛ²¹]   'float'

Reduplicated words which have reduplicated syllables beginning with an aspirated plosive do not show the low/high tone pattern as shown in (146).

(146) [mə³.kʰɔn⁵⁴.kʰɔn⁴².e²]   'sing'   [mə³².kʰɔn⁵²]   'song'
     [ju̯p³⁵.kʰɔk³².kʰɔk²¹.e²]   'snore'

Tone sandhi due to positional variants. Tone change often occurs when a specific morpheme or morpheme type is used adjacent to another specific morpheme or morpheme type. These alternations can be idiosyncratic or regular in nature. Yi-Burmese languages have been shown to exhibit tone sandhi between numerals and classifiers (Bradley 1971:12), between nouns and adverbializers (Matisoff 1973a:30), between vocatives and nonvocatives, between verbs and derived nouns (Matisoff 1974:159), and between negatives and their complements (Diehl 1993). Tibetan shows tonal variation based on syllable position in the word and in relation to stressed syllables (Mazaudon 1976:82, Duanmu 1993, Edmondson et al. 1995). Okell (1979) reports positional tone sandhi in Maru in which there are two classes of verbal particles which he calls 'raisers' and 'non-raisers'. The raisers raise the tone on the preceding verb one step while the non-raisers do not.

Zaiwa does have tonal variation describable as tone sandhi dependent on a particular morpheme adjacent to the affected syllable. Xu and Xu (1984) discuss five types as mentioned in §2.7. An example case can be demonstrated by adding a plural suffix to nouns. Nouns with a 31 or 4 tone change to 53 when followed by the plural suffix /be⁴/ as shown in (147).

(147) [dʑɔŋ⁴¹.dzɔ³¹]   'student'   [dʑɔŋ⁴¹.dzɔ⁵⁴.be³]   'students'
       [wuŋ³¹]   'wildcat'   [wuŋ⁵³.be³²]   'wildcats'
       [hup³.bu⁴]   'long root   [hup³.bu⁵⁴.be³]   'long root
                        vegetable'   vegetables'

6.4 Tone in checked syllables

In this book, tone in checked syllables is defined as a single tone with the actual form dependent on rules making use of the laryngeal features of the initial consonant and the voice quality, as discussed in §4.4. The allophonic variants of checked tone are shown in the chart in (148).

(148) CECIL tone traces for [pɨk⁵⁴.e²] 'kick' (upper) and [bɨk³².e¹²] 'shoot' (lower)[102]

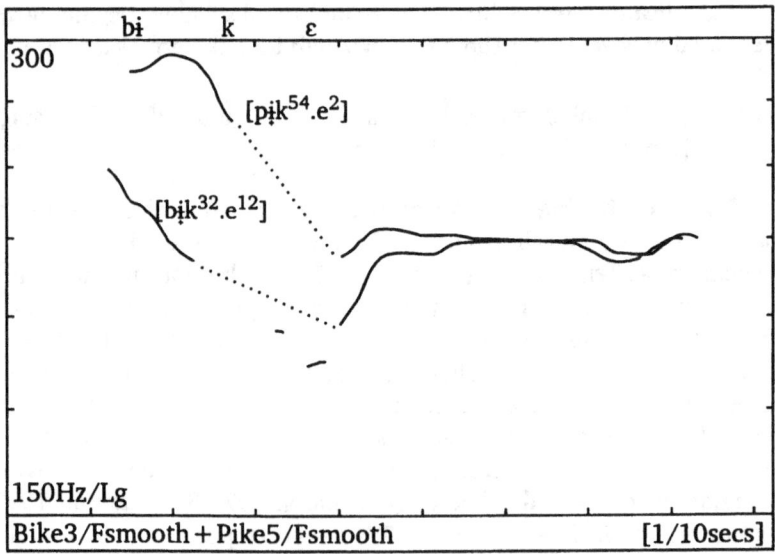

---

[102]The dotted lines connect the tone plots for the verb roots to the tone plots for the corresponding verbal particles.

This position follows Burling (1967), who gives checked tones their own identity as a single tone with allotones dependent on C_i and voice quality, separate from the falling tones. Burling states that:

> Atsi syllables which are terminated with a stop, whether /p, t, k or ʔ/, can all be considered to have a single tone, and the tone need not be indicated by a special mark beyond the sign for the stop. Phonetically, however, there are a number of variations among these, depending upon the initial consonant of the syllable. If the initial consonant is /s, ʃ, h/, or one of the voiceless aspirated series of stops, the vowels of stopped syllables are high, clear and very short. If the initial consonant belongs to the glottalized series, the vowel has a particularly strong 'creaky' quality and a high pitch which is terminated by the stop. If the initial consonant of the syllable is /v, j, l/, or a voiced (plain) stop, nasal or affricate, the vowel is both lower in pitch and longer than in the other cases, and the vowel is pronounced clearly with no "creaky" quality. (1967:19)[103]

A second possible option for tone assignment in checked syllables would be to analyze the high tone in checked syllables as a variant of the high falling (53) tone in unchecked syllables, and to analyze the mid tone in checked syllables as a variant of the mid falling (31) tone in unchecked syllables.

Support for this second account comes from three arguments. First, theoretical simplicity: assigning the same tones to unchecked and checked syllables simplifies the analysis. Only three tones are needed instead of three tones in unchecked syllables and a single tone with allotonic variants in checked syllables. Secondly, phonetic similarity: CECIL pitch plots show the checked and unchecked tones to be nearly identical in reference to height and fall at corresponding syllable lengths. Tone in checked syllables is prone to a slight fall and downdrift just as the tones in unchecked syllables are. Finally, phonological co-occurrence phenomena: the co-occurrence of initial consonant and voice quality with the corresponding tone in checked syllables does show a pattern, but it is not universal in the corpus of data for this study. The data for this study has the C_i/voice quality/tone correspondences in checked syllables shown in the table in (149).

---

[103] In my data, aspirated affricates tend to pattern with aspirated stops.

(149) Percentage of high and mid tones in checked syllables with
the indicated C_is or tense voice quality

Segmental/voice quality environment	Tone in checked syllables (%)	
	High	Mid
C_i /s ʃ h pʰ tʰ kʰ tsʰ tsʃʰ/	92	8
/tense voice quality/	94	6
C_i /m n ŋ l ɹ j w b d g dz dʒ/	10	90

For example, this table shows that syllables with a [+spread vf] C_i carry a high tone ninety-two percent of the time. The percentages indicated do argue for a high correspondence between type of C_i and tone, and voice quality and tone, but not a complete correspondence. In other research I have conducted on Maru and Lashi, both Tibeto-Burman languages closely related to Zaiwa, I have found that there is a two-way tone contrast in stopped syllables. Whether Maru and Lashi are historically conservative or whether intrusive final stops are involved, as stated by Burling (1966), is not clear. Nonetheless, the precedent exists for two stopped tones in Northern Burmic languages. A two-tone analysis would agree in principle with Maran's reinterpretation of Burling's Zaiwa tone system by combining high falling and high stopped tones into a unitary tone and by combining mid falling and mid stopped tones into a unitary tone. Maran (1971:93) comments that "This realignment gives the same tonal system for Atsi as Maru and Jinghpaw."

Therefore, we must ask whether Zaiwa tone in checked syllables should be considered a single tone based on the laryngeal features of the initial consonant and voice quality or, should it be considered two variants of the contrastive tones seen in unchecked syllables? Some scholars believe that tone in stopped syllables develops differently than tone in nonstopped syllables (Matisoff 1973b, Burling 1967). Others, however, do not agree. Mazaudon (1976:15) notes that "This view is commonly held, and seems to me very misleading. The checked syllables have no reason to behave in a basically different way from the smooth ones in a tonal split conditioned by initials." Benedict (1948:6) also addresses this issue; "Checked syllables (final stop) often show tonal features that differ somewhat from any found in unchecked syllables, but identification can be made in terms of phonetic similarity and pattern congruency." The question then remains, does Zaiwa have two or one lexical tone in checked syllables?[104]

---

[104] The existence of historical reasons for tone differences in checked and unchecked syllables, as discussed by Matisoff (1973b), Burling (1967), and Mazaudon (1976), will not be used as an argument for or against a single-tone analysis for tone in Zaiwa checked syllables. The jury seems to still be out on this issue.

It seems that the best way to support the analysis of a single tone in checked syllables is to state the reasons that are supportive of the one-tone analysis (my position) over the two-tone analysis and show why factors which support a two-tone analysis do not logically exclude a single-tone analysis. First, the reasons for supporting a single-tone analysis for checked syllables:

1. No contrast. There are no perfect contrastive tone pairs formed in checked syllables. The primary indicator of the existence of any phonological units in relation to other units is contrast. No such contrast is evident for tone in Zaiwa checked syllables.
2. Laryngeal features highly predictive of tone height. The patterns between C_i, voice quality, and tone in checked syllables, as shown in (147), give overwhelming evidence for the existence of a high correlation between the laryngeal features of C_i, voice quality, and tone height.
3. Phonetic motivation for a derivational analysis is strong. There is phonetic motivation for the occurrence of the observed allotones in checked syllables as discussed in §§3.4.3 and 3.4.5.

By contrast, three factors were presented which seem to argue for a two-tone analysis of tone in checked syllables. These factors, however, do not exclude a single-tone argument and are questionable in and of themselves when examined more closely:

1. Simplicity. A two-tone analysis of tone in Zaiwa checked syllables may seem to be simpler in relation to the complexity of tonal processes. Both analyses, however, still have only three contrastive tones. In the single-tone analysis, tone in checked syllables is predictable and does not contribute to the complexity of the lexical tone system. Therefore, simplicity does not differentiate effectively between the two treatments.
2. Analogous tone fall in both checked and unchecked syllables. The partial tone fall in checked syllables looks as if it could be a variant of the phonemic falling tones in unchecked syllables. The tone fall in checked syllables, however, was explained in §6.3.1 and is expected for the allotones in checked syllables.
3. The lack of universal correspondence between C_i, voice quality, and tone height. The occurrence of syllables which are contraindications of a single-tone analysis (~eight per cent in my corpus of data) can be explained as speaker variation, possible assimilation to words in context, and the possibility of intrusive final stops in Zaiwa as is the case in Maru. The low incidence of nonaligned syllables is not enough to argue for the two-toned analysis.

The support for a single-tone analysis of tone in Zaiwa checked syllables and the lack of evidence against the single-tone argument from the two-tone argument leads to the interpretation of a single tone in Zaiwa checked syllables with allotones conditioned by the laryngeal features of C_i and voice quality as discussed in §4.4.

6.5 Tone contrasts

Contrast between Zaiwa tones is shown in the table in (150).

(150) Contrast between Zaiwa tones

53 high falling tone	4 high-mid level tone	31 mid falling tone	2 low tone
[mjaŋ⁵³.ɛ³²] 'concerning horses'	[mjaŋ³.ɛ³] 'long time'	[mjaŋ³¹.e¹²] 'see'	
[ŋa̰m⁵³.e³¹] 'delicious'	[ŋam³.e³] 'cold (object)'	[ŋam³¹.e²] 'salty'	
[ʔi⁵³] '(kinship prefix)'	[ʔi̠⁴] 'two'	[ʔi³¹] 'penis'	
[wi⁵³.ɛ³¹] 'difficult'	[wi³⁴] 'fish sedative'	[wi³¹.ɛ²] 'smile'	
[biŋ⁵³.ɛ³¹] 'grill'	[biŋ³⁴.ɛ⁴³] 'full'	[biŋ³¹.ɛ¹²] 'sore muscles'	
[ɹa⁵².ɛ²¹] 'have business to do'	[ɹa³.ɛ³] 'smooth'	[ɹa³¹] 'one (count number)'	
	[ʔa⁴] '(vocative prefix)'		[ʔa²] '(negative prefix)'
[ʔa̰ṵ⁵³.mʔ³¹] 'mother-in-law'			[ʔa̰ṵ¹².mʔ³] 'big pot'

Contrast is established between the tones 53, 4, and 31 in open syllables and in syllables closed by a nasal. The final two rows show possible contrast of lexical tones with a low tone. This will be discussed in §6.6.

6.6 Low tone

Matisoff (1989a) differentiates between core and marginal phonological features in the Lahu syllable, including nasalization, segments created by borrowing, and a rare high rising tone.[105] He comments on the rare tone:

> There is much evidence to suggest that it is the lexically rarer tones in a language which are typically exploited for special jobs: in morphophonemic processes, in incompletely assimilated loanwords, or for affective/symbolic purposes. The relatively low functional load of a rare tone ensures that these special tasks will not overburden the system by creating large numbers of new homophones—and the salience afforded by their very rarity makes them appropriate for grammatical or symbolic duty. (1989:155)

Low tone has the lowest incidence of all tones in Zaiwa with only five examples (one-half percent of total) of unambiguous low tone morphemes. 'Unambiguous' here means, those syllables which do not have low tone due to tone assimilation or downdrift. Two occurrences of low tone are roots ([$ʔau^{21}$] 'pot' and [$bə^1.mau^1$] 'beard'), two are stressed prefixes ([$ʔa^2$] (negative) and [$ʔa^2$] 'relation to father'), and one is a reduced syllable ([$lə^2$] 'half'). No common 'grammatical or symbolic' duty can be assigned to the Zaiwa low tone paralleling that described by Matisoff for Lahu. Most other cases of phonetic low tone can be shown to be mid falling or high-mid level tones which have undergone tone sandhi alternations. Other cases, such as low tone in checked syllables, all begin with a voiced C_i, which correlates with lower tone in checked syllables. These morphemes may have been historically prenasalized, increasing synchronic voicing and the lowering effect.[106] There is no contrast between the low tone and the mid falling tone. This opens the possibility that the phonetic tone 2 is a variant of tone 31, but with a great deal of variation in pronunciation due to stress differences. The reduced syllables are unstressed which may induce lower tone. The stressed prefixes and roots could be true low tone, but a four-tone system would deviate from Maru, a closely related language with a three-tone system. Therefore, due to its low occurrence and questionable existence as an independent tone, low tone will be considered subphonemic in this analysis.

---

[105]In Lahu the high rising tone has a diminutive function.

[106]Comparison with the proto-language for prenasalized stops did not prove fruitful since occurrences of the lexical items in Zaiwa did not correspond with the lexical items proposed for the proto-forms.

6.7 Stress and tone

Tone in Tibeto-Burman languages can change due to differing stress on syllables. The effect can be small and not great enough to create contrastive tone changes, or large, causing tonal variance. Zaiwa has two major stress types and a third which can be added depending on the speaker's situation. Normal, or unmarked, stress is the stress applied to nonreduced syllables which carry contrastive tone. Weak stress or non-stress is applied to reduced syllables, such as historically reduced prefixes (giving iambic word meter) and verb-final suffixes (giving trochaic word meter). The third type of stress is an indicator of emotional emphasis. The interaction between stress and tone on reduced syllables was discussed in §6.2. The interaction between weak stress and tone and stress for emotional emphasis will be discussed here.

Verb-final suffixes are unstressed, which causes associated tones to be more prone to assimilation to the preceding tone.[107] This is similar to what Chelliah (1991:65) claims for Manipuri: "at both an underlying and a surface level, suffixes have no tone associated to them; instead, the pitch values observed for suffixes are simply the phonetic realization of stem tone to the right edge of the word." The unstressed suffixes in Zaiwa follow the tone rules for stressed syllables as shown in §6.3, but the tone on unstressed syllables tends to fall or be affected to extremes by the preceding tone. For example, the perfective aspect suffix /e⁴/ falls following a high falling tone (151a), and stays level following a level tone (151b), as expected. However, when /e⁴/ is preceded by a mid falling tone, its own tone begins at the level of the end of the preceding fall (see (151c) and the chart in (152)). This is in contrast to a level 4 tone in a stressed syllable following a mid falling tone, which begins at its normal tone height (see (151d) and the chart in (151)).

(151) a. [biŋ^{53}.ɛ^{31}]   /biŋ^{53}e^{4}/   'grill'
       b. [biŋ^{34}.ɛ^{43}]   /biŋ^{4}e^{4}/   'full'
       c. [biŋ^{31}.ɛ^{12}]   /biŋ^{31}e^{4}/   'sore (muscles)'
       d. [ban^{32}.bɔ^{3}]   /ban^{31}bɔ^{4}/   'flower'

---

[107] Matisoff (1989b:166) addresses unstressed particles in Lahu saying, "Once its initial consonant has disappeared, a functor is so phonologically slight that it may be helpless to resist the pull of the voracious, fully-stressed noun or verb that precedes it. If circumstances are right the functor's vowel and/or tone may be incorporated bodily into the vowel of the head-syllable, resulting in a complex, fused vocalic nucleus that is 'a-mora-and-a-half' long."

Zaiwa Suprasegmental Phonology

(152) CECIL tone trace of [biŋ³¹.ε¹²] /biŋ³¹e⁴/ 'sore (muscles)'

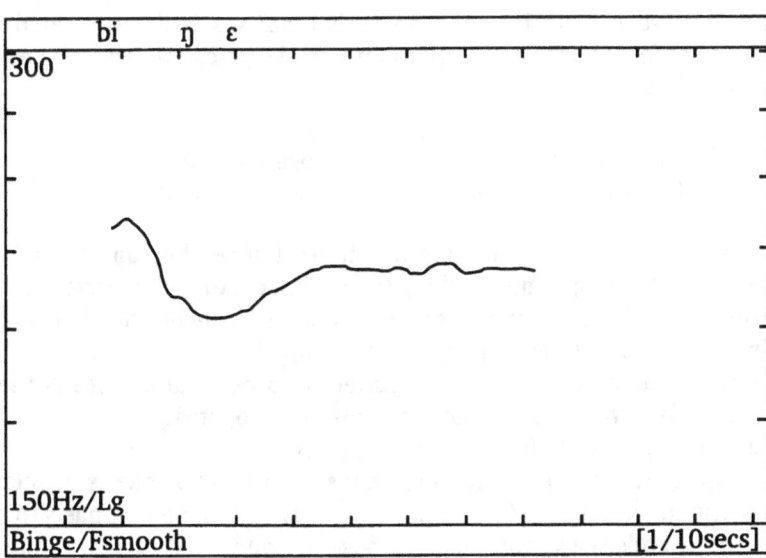

Note that the tone for the unstressed verbal suffix /e⁴/ begins at the height of the end of the full tone fall on the previous morpheme.

(153) CECIL tone trace of [ban³².bɔ³] /ban³¹bɔ⁴/ 'flower'

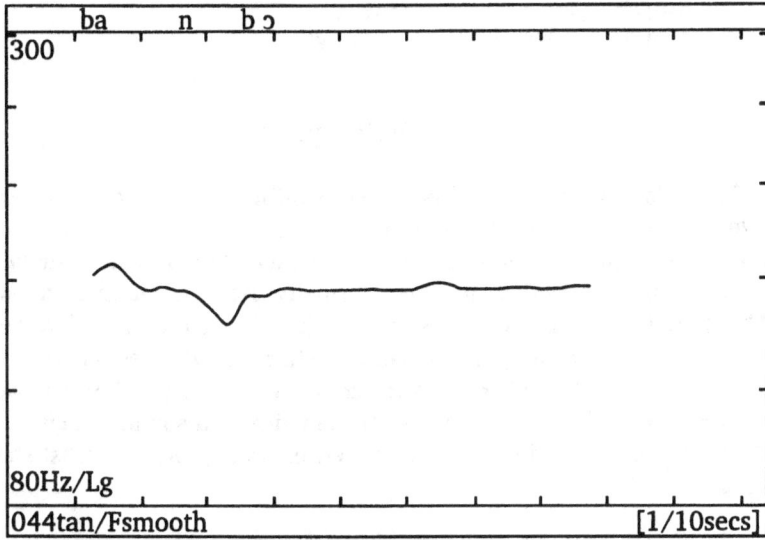

Note that the tone on the first syllable only falls slightly and the tone on the second syllable begins rather abruptly at a level 3.

The ease of assimilation may lead observers to believe that unstressed, verb-final suffixes are toneless. This view is countered by three observations. First, contrastive tone on verbal suffixes is demonstrated by the verbal suffixes /ɹa⁴/ (indicative) and /ɹa³¹/ (irrealis). Note the examples shown in (154).

(154) [nji̥³¹.ɹa¹²]   /nji̥³¹ɹa⁴/   'located^(indicative)'
       [nji̥³².ɹa²¹]   /nji̥³¹ɹa³¹/   'located^(irrealis)'

Both tones in the unstressed suffixes follow the tone variations expected following a mid falling tone.¹⁰⁸ Secondly, the perfective aspect suffix /e⁴/, tends to rise towards its phonemic level after being lowered by a preceding tone, e.g., [biŋ³¹.ɛ¹²] /biŋ³¹e⁴/ 'sore (muscles)'. Finally, in some cases, the tone on the perfective aspect suffix does not fall to a level 1 following a 53, which indicates its propensity to stay close to the level 4, e.g., [dɔ⁵³.ɛ³²] /dɔ⁵³e⁴/ 'set aside'.

The third area of interaction between stress and tone is in relation to emotional emphasis. When a speaker adds emotional emphasis to a statement, it adds stress and tends to raise the pitch and increase loudness as shown in (155).

(155) [ŋat³².e³]   'to bite'
       [kʰui³¹.ŋat⁵.e³]   'the dog bit (him)! with an emotional
                                emphasis'
       [mjɔ³².mjɔ²¹]   'many'
       [mjɔ⁵³.dɪk³.be³².ɛ²¹]   'too many!'

6.8 Voice quality

Many languages in Southeast Asia exhibit some form of contrast between two or more types of voice quality. Zaiwa is no exception. Tense voice contrasts with modal voice in Zaiwa. Modal voice includes the range of fundamental frequencies normally used in speaking and singing. The domain of voice quality is the syllable. Tense and modal voice occur with all tones and in open, closed, and checked syllables. Zaiwa speakers can identify the tense/modal voice contrast. One of the Zaiwa informants who provided this data described tense voice as a sound which "uses the throat more." Note the examples of tense/modal voice contrast shown in (156).

---

¹⁰⁸See (151c) and associated explanation, and (136) for details of tone change.

(156) Tense/modal voice contrasts in Zaiwa

    Tense voice   Modal voice

Tense voice		Modal voice	
[dʒa̰ŋ⁵³.e³²]	'near'	[dʒaŋ⁵³.e³²]	'hire out'
[kjṵʔ⁵⁴.ɛ²]	'dry'	[gjuʔ³².e³]	'afraid'
[ja̰m⁵³.e³²]	'thin object'	[jam⁵¹]	'time'
[mja̰ŋ³¹.e²]	'tall'	[mjaŋ³¹.e²]	'see'

The actual type of voice quality distinctions present in Zaiwa have been interpreted differently in the past. According to Burling (1967), Zaiwa shows a creaky/clear voice contrast. Burling states that historically laryngealization, or creaky voice, is a relic of proto-Tibeto-Burman preglottalized initials, and the initial is used to define the marked voice quality apparent in Zaiwa. More recently, however, creaky voice has been differentiated from the voice quality of tense voice. Tense voice is actually a high degree of overall muscular tension throughout the vocal system (Laver 1980:141). This high tension on the vocal folds creates a "tight" vocal quality.

> A tense voice will tend to have these characteristics: ligamental, harsh or ventricular phonation which will sound comparatively louder and higher-pitched; higher sub-glottal air pressure; slightly raised larynx; constriction of the upper larynx and lower pharynx, and possibly of the faucal pillars; a tensed velum; vigorous and extensive radial movements of the convex-surfaced tongue in segmental articulation; vigorous activity of the lips; and a more mobile jaw. (1980:154–55)

In contrast, creaky voice is a phonatory setting in which the vocal folds are more lax and thick with only a small length of the ligamental glottis in vibration at a low frequency, allowing air to "bubble" through the anterior end of the glottis (p. 125).

Zaiwa actually exhibits a tense voice quality rather than a creaky voice quality. The Zaiwa language informants who contributed to this study definitely exhibited the tight, higher frequency sound of tense voice rather than the bubbly sound of creaky voice. This difference can also be shown acoustically. Edmondson (1993) used an inverse filtering method with modified CECIL software and hardware in order to determine the state of the glottis in various words spoken by a Zaiwa speaker in

Southern China. His laryngeogram, shown in (157),[109] suggests that Zaiwa exhibits a tense/modal contrast and not a creaky/clear contrast.

(157) A composite plot of Zaiwa [ta̰⁵³] 'to hold hands (of a walking infant)' (lower waveform) versus [ta⁵³] 'to want' (upper waveform)

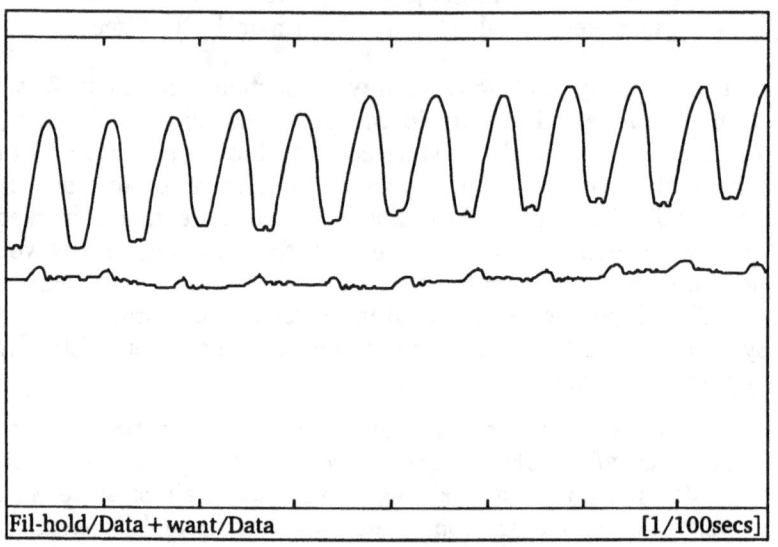

| Fil-hold/Data + want/Data | [1/100secs] |

Edmondson (1993:2) states that "The languages Zaiwa and Bela, turned out to have glottograms of a type that would be predicted for languages having the tense–lax voice contrast..."[110]

The distribution of tense voice and its affect on various segments of the syllable help to reveal certain laryngeal characteristics of tense voice. Tense voice does not occur in syllables with [+spread vf] initials, i.e., /pʰ tʰ kʰ tsʰ tʃʰ ʃ s h/. This is due to the fact that different phonatory and tension settings compete for the same parts of the larynx, making some settings incompatible with one another. Aspirated stops and affricates

---

[109]The tense/lax distinction shown in the plot is distinguished by the difference in distance between the wave and baseline (indicating the steady state egressive airflow leaving the mouth) and the length of the closed phase of the wave (indicating the varying air pressure wave of glottal vibration). Lax voice has a longer distance between the wave and baseline (corresponding to a more lax, open glottis) and a shorter closed phase of the wave (corresponding to more lax vocal folds allowing longer vibration periods). Tense voice has a shorter distance between the wave and baseline (corresponding to a more tense, closed glottis) and a longer closed phase of the wave (corresponding to tense vocal folds with shorter vibration periods) (Edmondson 1995). The voiceless [t] in [ta] in this example corresponds to a [d] in my transcription.

[110]Bela is a language closely related to Zaiwa, located in Yunnan, China.

and voiceless fricatives require a spread glottis, and tense voice requires a constricted glottis. The incompatibility is obvious. If tense voice is an artifact of historically preglottalized segments, then segments with inherent [+spread vf] features would not likely be included in the historical grouping.

On the other hand, certain phonatory settings and vocal processes can overlap, using the same part or state of the larynx at the same time, making them compatible. Compatibility can be demonstrated for voicing of sonorants with tense voice. Zaiwa tense voice is heard most clearly on vowels and to a lesser extent on nasals, glides, and liquids. Voicing of sonorants can occur with the glottis in the tense voice state, provided there is an increase in subglottal pressure to overcome vocal fold stiffness and constriction (Laver 1980:152). In tense syllables, all sonorants in Zaiwa remain voiced.

Zaiwa also demonstrates an intermediate stage of compatibility between phonation type and segmental features. Voiced plosive initials are devoiced in tense syllables. Voicing and tenseness are allowed to co-occur in sonorants, but the increased subglottal pressure necessary to allow voicing necessitates a period of 'start-up' time in which the pressure is built up enough to vibrate the stiff and constricted vocal folds. Due to the short duration of the plosive and the oral closure, which provides a back pressure, voicing does not occur with syllable-initial plosives. Using the same argument, voiced affricates are only partially voiced in tense syllables. The length of the affricate is approximately twice that of the plosive, but the subglottal pressure can only build up sufficiently for voicing during the fricative portion of the release. Fricatives allow impeded airflow and are, therefore, more compatible with voicing than either plosives or affricates. See §5.3.2 for further discussion of affricate voicing.

Tense voice/voicing compatibility can be displayed as a continuum from more sonorant segments down to less sonorant segments as shown in (158).

(158)   High tense voice/voicing   Low tense voice/voicing
                 compatibility   compatibility
          more sonorant ←---------------------------------→ less sonorant
                    vowels glides fricatives affricates plosives
                                  nasals
                                  liquids

Sonority correlates with the openness of the oral or nasal tract, allowing air to pass freely. The less back pressure there is due to constriction, the more pressure there is on the vocal folds from the air passing the vocal folds, which causes vibration. This helps to explain the varying effects of tense voice on voiced segments. The more sonority a segment manifests, the more compatible it is to voicing with tense voice, and the easier tense voice can be heard.

Tense voice occurs with all tones in unchecked syllables and correlates with the incidence of high tone in checked syllables as discussed in §§4.4 and 6.4. The analysis of voice quality in a system with tone may proceed in several different ways. The analysis depends on how the voice quality is integrated into the syllable. Bradley (1979:38) observes in Akha that "there are contrastive phonation-type differences of voice quality, which are realized simultaneously with the entire syllable, and thus there are initial, medial, and final phonetic features which can be attributed to this register distinction." Linguists have assigned voice quality distinctions to all different parts of the syllable. For example, Burling (1967) assigns voice quality distinctions in Zaiwa to the initial consonant based on a historical preglottalized series. Maddieson and Ladefoged (1985:437), working with Tibeto-Burman languages, chose to assign the tense/lax distinction to the vowel due to the fact that the major phonetic distinctions are heard on the vowel, although they do acknowledge other possible interpretations. Hu Tan and Dai Qingxia (1964) assign voice quality origin to the final vowel in some Tibeto-Burman languages. Another approach would be to assign voice quality to the syllable as a whole. Further variations are discussed in §3.4.4.

In addition to the different possibilities for the assignment of tense voice in the syllable, the question of the assignment of tone in relation to tense voice must be addressed. Voice quality and tone may be independent, dependent, or partially dependent. An independent assignment of tone and voice quality occurs when tone and voice quality do not interact and are marked separately. An example of a dependent assignment of tone and voice quality is the analysis of Black Lahu by Lewis (1968) in which he combined voice quality and tone in order to allow for a single symbol to be used to mark combinations of voice quality and tone in the orthography. A partially dependent assignment would allow for an independent assignment of tone and voice quality in some cases, while in other cases a dependent assignment is made.

In addition to the place of assignment in the syllable and the assignment in relation to tone, the manner of assignment is also debatable. Is the voice quality considered an inherent feature of a segment, or is it an autosegment which exists on a separate tier? Combining the options for the assignment of tense voice to the syllable, the assignment of tense voice in relation to tone, and the manner of association, a chart can be constructed showing twenty-four possibilities or types for the assignment of tense voice as shown in (159).

(159) Voice quality in relation to tone

Manner of association	Assignment in syllable	Independent	Dependent	Partially dependent
autosegmental	C_i	1	2	3
segmental		4	5	6
autosegmental	vowel	7	8	9
segmental		10	11	12
autosegmental	C_f	13	14	15
segmental		16	17	18
autosegmental	whole syllable	19	20	21
segmental		22	23	24

The particular assignment for voice quality is best made using language-specific factors, both diachronic and synchronic. This analysis of Zaiwa takes an autosegmental approach to suprasegmentals, and, therefore, the manner of assignment is autosegmental by choice. Voice quality has been shown to be independent of tone in unchecked syllables and to have a dependent relationship in checked syllables where tone depends on initial consonant voicing and voice quality. Therefore, a partially-dependent assignment of voice quality is chosen depending on the interaction with tone in different syllable types. Finally, there is historical evidence that would lead to the assignment of voice quality to both the syllable-initial consonant and the syllable-final consonant (see §4.2). Voice quality is assigned to C_i in this analysis since nothing is gained from assignment to both C_i and C_f, and a consistent assignment to C_i provides a more straightforward analysis. It should be noted that assignment, in the sense used here, really means initial association of the autosegment for voice quality to C_i. The assignment of voice quality to C_i is not complete, however, since the tense voice quality is heard across the syllable. An autosegmental approach allows the tense voice quality to spread across the entire syllable and still show independence from or dependence with tone, as shown in §4.4. An autosegmental analysis also does away with the need for a glottalized series of stops, affricates, nasals, glides, and liquids, as suggested by Burling (1967) to account for the voice quality. A single autosegment can replace the additional series, cutting the phonemic consonant inventory by nearly half.

The discussion above shows that voice quality assignment in Zaiwa is type 3 in (159), with a relationship to type 21 after voice quality spreads over the syllable. The vast number of possibilities for voice quality assignment when simply considering three factors which may affect the analysis helps to show the increase in complexity of language analysis and representation when more than one suprasegmental must be taken into account.

6.9 Conclusion

The primary contributions of this study are in the area of tone and voice quality representation and analysis. In chapter 4, an autosegmental framework for the analysis and representation of Zaiwa tone and voice quality was developed incorporating underspecification and a laryngeal feature geometry. The framework was utilized to represent lexical and derived tone in Zaiwa. The analysis of derived tone showed that initial consonant voicing is not a critical feature for determining tone height in checked syllables, while the association and spread of the glottal features [+/−spread vf], [+/−stiff vf], and [+/−const vf] are responsible for the determination of tone at the surface level in checked syllables. In chapter 6, the suprasegmentals of tone and voice quality in Zaiwa were presented. The complexity inherent in systems with two interacting suprasegmental features (such as tone and voice quality) was discussed.

Several additional areas of particular interest were also presented. Four of them are summarized here.
1. Tone, glottal stop, and voice quality are underlyingly independent features in Zaiwa. Glottal stop has complete distribution with all tones and all voice quality distinctions. Tense voice has complete distribution with all tones.
2. The Zaiwa complex onset may interact with the rhyme to increase syllable weight. A complex onset forces the reinterpretation of the diphthong /ui/ as a bisyllabic series instead of breaking the bimoraicity constraint.
3. Six underlying types of word-initial CV syllables were discussed (§5.2.5) based on historical origin and synchronic phonological features. These six underlying forms were reduced to three presenting surface forms in Zaiwa.
4. Tone in Zaiwa checked syllables was discussed (§6.4) as a single-tone versus a two-tone process. The evidence presented led to a single-tone interpretation of pitch in Zaiwa checked syllables.

Several questions concerning phonological processes in Zaiwa and other Tibeto-Burman languages were addressed in this study, but not sufficiently resolved. These issues would be interesting to pursue through further research. I will list five of them.
1. Independent control versus dependent production of pitch in relation to consonant voicing as discussed in §3.4.3. Tibeto-Burman languages show a complete range of correlation between tone and consonant voicing. Within the same language family, voicing and pitch can range from being independently controlled to complete dependency. A question for further research is, "What is the mechanism by which

independent versus dependent voicing and tone height are produced in different languages?"

2. The independent control versus dependent production of pitch in relation to voice quality distinctions was discussed in §3.4.5. Voice quality differences correlate with tonal differences in many Tibeto-Burman languages. The wide range of voice quality interaction with tone within the same language family reveals an underlying independence of pitch and voice quality production with tendencies toward certain correlations. A question for further research is, "What is the mechanism by which pitch control and voice quality production are incorporated into a child's speech apparatus?"

3. Possible multiple origins for tense voice in Zaiwa and other Tibeto-Burman languages was discussed in §§3.4.4 and 4.2. The data in this study suggests that Zaiwa tense voice may come from historical preglottalized initials and loss of final stop features. These seemingly multiple origins need to be investigated. The possibility of multiple origins also leads to the possibility of different voice qualities as a result. A question for further research is, "What is (are) the origin(s) of voice quality in Zaiwa and, if multiple, what are the characteristics of the resulting voice qualities?"

4. The origins of voicing distinctions on syllable-initial stops and affricates was discussed in §5.3.1. Zaiwa seems to have heavily voiced, minimally voiced, and voiceless stops at the phonetic level. A study incorporating instrumental analysis in combination with historical analysis of these features may give clues to their origins and distinctions.

5. Devoicing versus deaspiration in tense voice syllables was discussed in §5.3.2. In Zaiwa, voiced stops syllable initially are devoiced in tense syllables. The literature for Hani and Akha, however, posit deaspiration of the initial stop in laryngealized syllables. Historically, the origin of laryngealization in Hani and Akha was the loss of final consonants with the transfer of laryngeal features to the remaining vowels. In Zaiwa, the origin of laryngealization may differ from that of Hani and Akha. A possible research question brought up by the differing processes is, "How do the origins for laryngealization uniquely affect segmental processes?"

The analysis of tone and voice quality presented in this study provides an account for many of the interactions observed in Zaiwa between prosodic features and between prosodic and segmental features. The analysis also encourages us to search for answers to the proposed questions. It is my hope that the information presented here will be of use to other linguists wrestling with similar problems in the study of the suprasegmentals, segmentals, and their interactions.

Appendix A
Further Details of Zaiwa Segmental Phonology

A.1 Consonantal contrasts

Labial contrasts

Labial consonants /pʰ b m w/ are shown in contrast in (160).

(160) pʰ   b   m   w

    [pʰi⁵².ɛ²¹]   [bi⁵³.ɛ³¹]   [mi⁵³.ɛ³²]   [wi⁵².ɛ²]
    'untie'   'give'   'to follow'   'difficult'

    [pʰʊt⁵⁴.ɛ³]   [bʊt³².ɛ³]   [mʊt³².ɛ³]   [wʊt³².ɛ³]
    'blacken in fire'   'dye'   'hungry'   'blow'

    [pʰjɔ⁵³]   [bjɔ³¹]   [mjɔʔ³¹]
    'cockroach'   'bee'   'grass'

    [pʰat⁵.e²]   [bat².e²³]   [wat²¹.e²]
    'vomit'   'hit'   'sore mouth'

                        [baŋ³⁴.dai⁵³]   [maŋ⁵².ɛ²¹]   [waŋ³¹.ɛ²]
                        'rabbit'   'old (person)'   'enter'

Nasal Contrasts

Nasal consonants /m n ŋ/ are shown in contrast in (161).

(161)   m   n   ŋ

[mɔ⁵³]   [nɔ⁵³]   [ŋɔ⁵⁴ʔ]
'that (lower)'   'nose'   'bird'

[mau³¹]   [nau²³]   [ŋau³².e²³]
'rain'   'mother's milk' 'weep'

[maŋ⁵².ɛ²¹]   [naŋ⁵³.ɛ³]
'old (person)'   '2sPOSS'

                 [na⁵³.ɛ³¹]   [ŋa⁵³.ɛ³²]
                 'drunk'   '1POSS'

Alveolar, alveopalatal, and palatal contrasts

Alveolar, alveopalatal, and palatal consonants /tʰ d tsʰ tʃʰ dz ʥ n s ʃ l r j/ are shown to be in contrast in (162)–(166).

(162) Alveolar Contrasts

tʰ   d   tsʰ   dz

[tʰu³².ɛ²]   [du⁵³.ɛ³¹]   [tsʰu⁴³.ɛ³]   [dzu³¹]
'thick'   'dig'   'fat'   'thorn'

[tʰɔʔ⁵⁴.ɛ³²]   [dɔʔ³².ɛ²¹]   [tsʰɔ³¹]   [dzɔ⁵³.ɛ²¹]
'sharp'   'climb up'   'salt'   'eat'

[tʰaŋ³¹]   [daŋ⁵³.e³¹]   [tsʰam⁵³]   [dzam³¹]
'fire-wood'   'fly'   'hair'   'bridge'

[tʰuŋ⁵¹]   [duŋ³¹]   [ʥun³¹]
'pocket'   'wing'   'guard'

Appendix A

(163) Alveolar and alveopalatal contrasts

tsʰ	tʃʰ	dz	ʤ
[tsʰɔ³¹] 'salt'	[tʃʰɔ³¹] 'hive'	[dzɔ⁵³.ɛ²¹] 'eat'	[ʤɔ⁵³.ɛ³¹] 'correct'
[tsʰam⁵³] 'hair'	[tʃʰaŋ³¹] 'ginger'	[dzam³¹] 'bridge'	[ʤaŋ⁵³.ɛ³²] 'hire out'
[tsʰə⁵⁴.wam⁵³] 'wall'	[tʃʰə⁴.pʰjɔ⁵³] 'mat'	[dzə³.ʔa̰ṵ⁵³] 'son-in-law'	[ʤə³².wɔ³¹] 'place'

(164)

tsʰ	s	ʃ	tʃʰ
[tsʰɔ³¹] 'salt'	[sɔ⁵².ɛ²¹] 'walk'	[ʃɔ⁵³] 'tongue'	[tʃʰɔ³¹] 'hive'
[tsʰu⁴³.ɛ³] 'fat'	[sum³⁵.wi⁵²] 'sand'	[ʃum⁵³.e³²] 'weave rope'	[tʃʰum³².e²³] 'stingy'
	[sʊt⁵⁴.ɛ²¹] 'wipe'	[ʃʊt⁵⁴.ɛ³²] 'wrong'	[tʃʰut⁵⁴.e²¹] 'take off'
[tsʰam⁵³] 'hair'		[ʃam⁵³] 'knife'	[tʃʰam⁵³.ɛ³¹] 'cold'

(165) Alveolar contrasts

l	ɹ	n
[ʔə³.luʔ³²] 'not enough'	[gə.³ɹu⁵³.ɛ²] 'shout'	[ŋa³.nuŋ³] '1PINCL'
[kʰət⁵.lam⁵³.ʃi³¹] 'eggplant'	[dzɔ³².ɹam³¹] 'young man'	[kʰə³.nam³⁴³.le³¹] 'often'
[la³.hɔi⁴] 'snail'	[ɹa³.kʰun⁴¹] 'that time'	
	[ɹa⁵².ɛ²¹] 'have business'	[na⁵³.ɛ³¹] 'drunk'

Aspects of Zaiwa Prosody

l	ɹ	n
[le³.ɛ³]		[ne³².ɛ²³]
'come'		'red'

(166) Alveopalatal and palatal contrasts

j	dʑ
[jɔ⁵³.ɛ³¹]	[dʑɔ⁵³.ɛ³¹]
'itch'	'correct'
[jaŋ³².mi²¹]	[dʑaŋ⁵³.e³²]
'wife'	'hire out'
[jap³¹.e²]	[dʑap⁵⁴.e³]
'stand'	'narrow'

Velar and labiovelar contrasts

Velar and labiovelar consonants /kʰ g ŋ w/ are shown in contrast in (167).

(167)

kʰ	g	ŋ	w
[kʰɔ⁵³.ɛ²¹]	[gɔ³.ɛ³]	[ŋɔ³¹]	[wɔ³².ɛ²]
'bitter'	'dance'	'1s'	'fall (rain)'
[kʰun⁵²]	[guŋ³¹]	[ŋun³¹]	[wuŋ⁴²]
'time'	'body'	'silver'	'wildcat'
[kʰi³¹]	[gi⁴³.ɛ³]		[wi⁵³.ɛʔ³²]
'excrement'	'skinny'		'those people'
[kʰat⁴.e²]		[ŋat³².e³]	[wat²¹.e²]
'drive out'		'bite'	'sore feeling in mouth from seeds'
	[gap⁵.e³]	[ŋap⁵⁴.e²]	[mi³².wap⁴]
	'dip in sauce'	'count'	'ashes'

Glottal contrasts

Relevant contrasts between glottal consonants and phonetically similar consonants /k^h ʔ h s/ are shown in (168).

(168)

k^h	ʔ	h	s
[k^{h}e^{31}.ɛ^{12}]	[ʔe^{31}.ɛ^2]	[he^{53}.ɛ^{31}]	[se^{53}.ɛ^{31}]
'encourage to do'	'went'	'that'	'know'
[k^{h}un^{51}]	[ʔu^{51}]	[hu^{53}]	[su^{52}]
'time (bound)'	'intestines'	'that (higher)'	'that person'
[k^{h}ɔ^{53}.ɛ^{21}]	[ʔɔ^{21}.ɛ^{13}]	[hɔ^{53}.ɛ^{21}]	[sɔ^{52}.ɛ^{21}]
'bitter'	'want'	'plant'	'walk'

A.2 Additional phonological processes affecting consonants

Devoicing and unreleasing

Plosives are voiceless, unaspirated, and unreleased word finally and are voiceless and unaspirated when syllable final and word internal. Syllable-final plosives are also co-articulated with a glottal stop. It is unclear whether the co-articulation is a phonetic addition caused by the position of the plosive in the syllable or whether the final plosives are historically derived from a unique stop series. In order to simplify synchronic analysis, the co-articulated stop/glottal stop will be considered to be allophonic with an existing plosive series.[111] It is not clear whether the syllable-final plosive series comes from the voiced or aspirated plosive series. Thus, there is neutralization of contrast between the aspirated and voiced plosive series syllable finally. The [+const vf] feature associated with the co-articulated stop/glottal stop disallows both voicing and aspiration. The voiced plosive series will be used to represent the final plosives in phonemic transcription to indicate the neutralization. Note the examples shown in (169).[112]

---

[111] It could be argued that the voiced plosives are closer phonetically (narrower glottal aperture) to the co-articulated stop/glottal stop series and, therefore, a better candidate to be the phonemic source. In actuality, the co-articulated stop/glottal stop most likely came from a historical reduction sequence with the following pattern: -b → -p → -p^ʔ → ʔ.

[112] The phonetic representation for unreleased is used in these examples to show the unreleased character of word final plosives. Elsewhere in phonetic transcription the word-final plosives are assumed unreleased but are not marked as such for convenience.

(169) [nɪk˺³²]   'bamboo shoot'
      [siŋ³².wap˺³]   'lungs'
      [hup³.buʔ]   'long root vegetable'

This analysis gives the rule shown in (170).[113]

(170)   C   → +const vf / __ $
      ⎡ −son ⎤
      ⎣ −cont ⎦

The glottal constriction of plosives syllable finally, word internally, explains the general lack of voicing assimilation between voiceless syllable-final plosives and the following voiced initials. The glottal constriction is enough to counteract the anticipation of voicing from following voiced segments due to incompatibility of glottal states.

Labial closure

The phonetic manifestation of the labial approximant /w/ depends on the speaker and the rate of speech. In slow speech the /w/ is generally pronounced as [w]. In normal speech the phonetic shape depends on the speaker. Two different speakers will be compared.[114]

Speaker 1: The labial approximant w tends to be in free variation with [βʷ] and [v] in certain environments and in complementary distribution in other environments. The labio-dental fricative v occurs preceding /u/ while w never does. This is an example of dissimilation. The segments [w] and [βʷ] are in free variation preceding /ɔ/. The segments [w], [βʷ] and [v] are in free variation preceding /a/. [w] is found elsewhere. Note the examples shown in (171). The rule for labial closure is shown in (172).

(171)   [vum³.gam⁵³]   [vun³².e²]
        'rattan'   'put strap on head'

        [βʷɔʔ³²] ~ [wɔʔ³²]   [βʷɔʔ³²ɛ³] ~ [wɔʔ³²ɛ³]
        'chicken'   'weave'

        [wa³¹] ~ [βʷa³¹] ~ [va³¹]
        'village'

---

[113]Distinctive features used in this section are found in appendix B.
[114]Speaker 1 is Mr. Tangun. Speaker 2 is Mrs. Roi Seng.

Appendix A

(172) /w/ → [v] / __ /u/
      [w] ~ [βʷ] / __ /ɔ/
      [w] ~ [βʷ] ~ [v] / __ /a/
      [w] elsewhere

Speaker 2: The allophones [w] and [βʷ] are in free variation preceding /i e/. [w] is found elsewhere. Note the examples shown in (173). This gives the rule for labial closure shown in (174).

(173) [nap̣⁴³.βʷiŋ²¹] ~ [nap̣⁴³.wiŋ²¹] 'snot'
      [mi³. βʷe³¹.ɛ¹] ~ [mi³.we³¹.ɛ¹] 'woman'

(174) /w/ → [w] ~ [βʷ] / __ V [−bk]
      [w] elsewhere

A.3 Vocalic contrasts

The vowel /i/, realized phonetically as [i ɪ], is shown to be in contrast with /e u i̡/ by the examples shown in (175).

(175) Vocalic contrasts with /i/

i			e	
[bi⁵³.ɛ³²]	'pay'		[be⁵³.ɛ³¹]	'already'
[nji³¹.ɛ²]	'have'		[nje³².ɛ³]	'hot'
[ʥi⁵².ɛ²¹]	'ride horse'		[ʥe³².ɛ³]	'arrive'

i			u	
[diŋ⁴.ɛ⁴³]	'straight'		[duŋ⁵³.ɛ²¹]	'ask for'
[bɪt³².ɛ³]	'break'		[bʊt³².ɛ³]	'dye'
[wi³².ɛ²³]	'buy'		[wu³⁴.ɛ³]	

i			i̡	
[nji⁴]	'day'		[nji̡³².ɛ²]	'live, dwell'
[mi⁵³.ɛ³²]	'question'		[mi̡⁵².ɛ²¹]	'to close'

The vowel /e/, realized phonetically as [e ɛ æ] is shown to be in contrast with /a u ɔ ẹ/ by the examples shown in (176)–(177).

(176) Vocalic contrasts with /e/

e		a	
[he³.ma³²]	'that there'	[ha⁵.dʒuŋ⁵²]	'what?'
[ne³².ɛ²³]	'red'	[na⁵³.ɛ³¹]	'drunk'
[be³]	'that'	[ba²³]	'plow'

e		u	
[tʰe⁵³.ɛ³²]	'peck'	[tʰu³².ɛ²]	'thick'
[geʔ³¹.ɛ²]	'wrap up'	[guʔ³².ɛ²]	'pick up'
[dʒe³.ɛ³]	'to (a time)'	[ʔa³².dʒu³.ɛ³]	'hate'

(177) Vocalic contrasts with /e/

e		ɔ	
[dʒe³.ɛ³]	'to (a time)'	[dʒɔ⁵³.ɛ³¹]	'correct'
[ne³².ɛ²³]	'red'	[nɔ³¹.ɛ²]	'sick'
[se⁵³.ɛ³¹]	'know'	[sɔ⁵².ɛ²¹]	'walk'

e		ę	
[njɛ³.ɛ³]	'hot'	[njɛ̨⁵³.ɛ³²]	'burn'
[lap⁴.pʰjɛt⁵⁴.e¹]	'lightning'	[pjɛ̨t⁴]	'duck'
[ge³¹.ɛ²]	'measure'	[kę⁵³.ɛ²¹]	'to measure'

The vowel /a/, realized phonetically as [a], is shown in contrast with /u ɔ ą/ in (178).

(178) Vocalic contrasts with /a/

a		u	
[tʰaŋ³¹]	'firewood'	[tʰuŋ⁵¹]	'pocket'
[tʃʰaŋ³¹]	'ginger'	[tʃʰuŋ³¹.e³]	'use'
[ʃam⁵³]	'knife'	[ʃum³²]	'woven rope'

a		ɔ	
[tʃʰam⁵³.ɛ³¹]	'cold'	[tʃʰɔm⁵³.e³¹]	'help'
[daŋ⁵³.e³¹]	'fly'	[dɔŋ³¹]	'hole'
[na⁵³.ɛ³¹]	'drunk'	[nɔ³¹.ɛ²]	'sick'

a		ą	
[wa³¹]	'village'	[wą⁵³]	'father'
[dʒaŋ⁵³.e³²]	'hire'	[dʒąŋ⁵³.e³²]	'near'

Appendix A

[mjaŋ³¹.e¹²]   'see'   [mjaŋ̰³¹.e¹²]   'tall'

The vowel /u/, realized phonetically as [u ʊ ɨ ɯ] is shown in contrast with /ɔ ṷ/ in (179).

(179) Vocalic contrasts with /u/

	u			ɔ	
[duŋ³¹]	'wing'		[dɔŋ³¹]	'hole'	
[gju?³².e³]	'afraid'		[gjɔ?³¹.ε¹²]	'cold (person)'	
[bju³¹]	'person'		[bjɔ³¹]	'bee'	

	u			ṷ	
[mjuŋ⁵³.ε³¹]	'tired'		[mjṵk⁵⁴.e²¹]	'bury'	
[nḭk⁵.lum³¹]	'heart'		[?ṵt³².lṵm³²]	'head'	
[nun⁴.e³]	'shake (int.)'		[nṵn⁵³.e³]	'to shake (tr.)'	

The vowel /ɔ/, realized phonetically as [ɔ], is shown in contrast with /ɔ̰/ in (180).

(180) Vocalic contrasts with /ɔ/

	ɔ			ɔ̰	
[nɔ⁵²]	'not sure'		[nɔ̰⁵³]	'nose'	
[gɔ⁵³.ε²¹]	'dance'		[kɔ̰⁵³.ε²]	'big'	
[lɔ³¹]	'large cat'		[lɔ̰³¹]	'trousers'	

The diphthongs /ai au ui ɔi/, realized phonetically as [ai au ui ɔi], respectively, are shown in contrast with each other in (181).

(181) Vocalic contrasts between diphthongs

	ai			au	
[mai³¹]	'mile'		[mau³¹]	'rain'	
[lai⁵³.ε³²]	'heavy'		[lau³².ε²³]	'cry'	
[ʃai³¹.ε²]	'different'		[ʃau⁴².ε²¹]	'less'	

	ai			ɔi	
[hai⁵³]	'what?'		[la³.hɔi⁴]	'snail'	
[kʰui³¹]	'dog'		[kʰɔi³.dze⁵¹]	'chopsticks'	

ai		ui	
[baŋ³.lai³¹]	'sea'	[nɔt³.lui³¹]	'buffalo'
[mə³.dʒɔ³⁴.mai⁵³]	'make'	[laŋ⁵³.mui³¹]	'snake'
[hai⁵³]	'what?'	[hui⁵³.ɛ²¹]	'meet'
		[kʰui³¹]	'dog'

au		ui	
[tʰau⁵².e²¹]	'stab'	[tʰui⁵³.ɛ²¹]	'hit'
[bau³¹]	'insect'	[bui³²]	'sun'
[ŋɔʔ⁵⁴.mau³¹]	'feather'	[nʊt⁵.mui³¹]	'beard on chin'

The diphthongs /ai au ui/ are shown in contrast with their tense voiced variants by the examples shown in (182).

(182) Modal tense

ai		a̰ḭ	
[baŋ³.lai³¹]	'sea'	[wi?³.la̰ḭ⁵³]	'boat'
[tʰai⁵⁴.lum⁵³.ɛ¹²]	'exchange'	[ta̰ḭ⁵³.ɛ²]	'tell'

au		a̰ṵ	
[mau³².bɔ³.ɛ³]	'bright'	[ma̰ṵ⁵².ɛ²]	'lie, fib'
[dau³.bi⁵³.ɛ21]	'return item'	[ta̰ṵ³¹.ɛ¹²]	'answer'

ui		ṵḭ	
[dui³⁴]	'leaf coat'	[tṵḭ⁵³.ɛ³¹]	'tie'
[mɪt³.wui³⁵².ɛ²¹]	'think hard'	[ʃə⁴³.wṵḭ³²]	'bone'

No modal/tense contrast between /ɔi/ and /ɔ̰ḭ/ was observed, most likely due to lack of data.

A.4 Additional phonological processes affecting vowels

Lowering

Lowering refers to the change of vowels from [+ATR] to [−ATR] in certain environments. There are three general lowering processes observed in the data which apply to more than one phoneme. Each process will be discussed briefly here.

The first lowering process is a result of palatal and/or alveopalatal consonants preceding front vowels, e.g., [njɛ³.ɛ³] 'hot' versus [nḛ³².ɛ²³]

Appendix A

'red'. The combination of the front vowel and the preceding palatal consonant, which is [+hi], tends to retract the tongue root. The reasons for this are unclear, as the opposite would be expected since [+hi] segments would tend to advance the tongue root.

The second process is a result of checking the syllable with an oral stop, e.g., [ʃut⁵⁴.ɛ³²] 'wrong' versus [ʃu?⁵.ɛ²] 'drink'. Maddieson (1985:449) states that in Tibeto-Burman, as well as other languages, "The occurrence of shorter and (usually) lower vowels in closed syllables is widespread." Maddieson goes on to explain that it is likely in a checked syllable that the vowel is affected by the transition from the initial consonant but in the open syllable the vowel is longer and much of it is beyond the influence of the initial consonant. The transition period between the initial consonant and the vowel in checked syllables is likely to lower the vowel. The oral features of syllable-final plosives, not the glottal features, must be responsible for helping to lower preceding vowels since the glottal stop does not have the same affect as oral stops. The longer vowel length associated with the glottal stop, as discussed in §6.3.1, may be responsible for a longer transition time, and hence, no perceivable lowering effect. In contrast to this process, high vowels tend to stay [+ATR] in checked syllables when preceded by palatal glides, and in some cases, when preceded by alveopalatal affricates which may be reinterpreted as a stop/glide combination, e.g., [mɪt³.ɛ³] 'think' versus [mjik³] 'sprout', and [sut⁵⁴.ɛ²¹] 'wipe' versus [ʥut⁵.ɛ²] 'slippery'. The reason for an absence of lowering when the vowels in checked syllables are preceded by a [+hi] segment may be due to what Duanmu (1991:153) calls articulatory enhancement in which "[+hi] and [+atr] tend to co-occur because both features move the tongue in the same direction." The first and second processes sometimes work in combination.

The third process is the lowering of [−bk] vowels by a syllable-final [n], e.g., [kʰɪ⁴²n.ɛ³] 'choose' versus [kʰi⁵³ŋ] 'o'clock'. The motivation for this process is not clear, but it may be due to tongue placement constraints for a front vowel followed by a coronal nasal.

In light of these general tendencies, we will now discuss allophonic processes related to specific vowel phonemes. The vowel [ɪ] is an allophone of /i/. [ɪ] occurs in syllables checked by an oral plosive when not preceded by /j/ as shown in (183) which leads to the rule shown in (184).

(183) [ʥɪt⁵⁴.ɛ³²]   'love'   [tḭ?⁵⁴.ɛ³²]   'small'
       [mɪt³.ɛ³]   'think'   [mjik³]   'sprout'
       [bɪt³.gjɔ⁴³.ɛ²] 'fall'   [bjit³².ɛ³]   'break rope'
       [wi³.tʃʰɪk⁵.ɛ²] 'laugh'   [pʰjik⁵.ɛ²¹] 'spicy'

(184) /i/ → [ɪ] / C (not [j]) __ $\begin{bmatrix} -\text{cont} \\ -\text{son} \end{bmatrix}$ (not [ʔ]$)

[ɪ] occurs in open syllables with an alveopalatal affricate or alveopalatal fricative onset preceding [−cont], obstruent onsets of the following syllable as shown in (185).

(185) [ʃɪ³.ʥi⁴]   'seed'   [ʃi⁴.ma⁴³]   'here'
      [ha⁵⁴.tʃʰɪ³².tʃʰi⁵².ɛ²] 'sneeze'   [kʰji⁵⁴.bu³]   'calf'

This leads to the rule shown in (186).

(186) /i/ → [ɪ] / $ $\begin{bmatrix} +\text{high} \\ -\text{back} \\ +\text{strid} \end{bmatrix}$ __ $ $\begin{bmatrix} -\text{cont} \\ -\text{son} \end{bmatrix}$

[ɪ] also occurs in syllables closed by an /n/ as shown in (187) which leads to the rule shown in (188).

(187) [ʃɪn³¹]   'louse'   [ʃiŋ³².gan³².ma²³] 'outside'
      [mjɪn³⁴]   'night'   [mjiŋ³¹]   'name'
      [kʰɪn⁴².ɛ³]   'choose'   [kʰiŋ⁵³]   'o'clock'

(188) /i/ → [ɪ] / __ $\begin{bmatrix} +\text{nas} \\ +\text{ant} \end{bmatrix}$

The vowel [i] does not occur in these environments.
The vowel [ɛ] is an allophone of /e/. [ɛ] occurs preceding an oral plosive and in word-final syllables checked by a /ʔ/ as shown in (189) which leads to the rule shown in (190).

(189) [dɛk³¹.ɛ²]   'measure'   [mɛ³².bu³¹]   'clothing'
      [laŋ⁵².tʃʰeʔ³².ɛ¹] 'tear paper'   [tęʔ⁵³.ɛ²]   'wet (clothes)'
      [ban³².ʥaŋ³⁴.ʃɛʔ⁴¹] 'finished'   [jaŋ³¹.ɛʔ¹²]   'with him'

(190) /e/ → [ɛ] / __ $\begin{bmatrix} -\text{cont} \\ -\text{son} \end{bmatrix}$ (not ʔ)
      __ ʔ#

[ɛ] occurs following /j/ as shown in (191) which leads to the rule shown in (192).

(191) [njɛ³.ɛ³]   'hot'   [nę³².ɛ²³]   'red'

(192) /e/ → ɛ/ [j] __

[ɛ] occurs preceding /n/ in closed syllables as shown in (193) which leads to the rule shown in (194).

(193) [tsʰam⁵³.dzɛn⁴³.ɛ³²] 'cut hair'   [seŋ⁴.pʰɔ⁵.ʃi³¹] 'papaya'
      [dʑɛn⁵³.ɛ³¹]   'filter'   [dʑe³².ɛ³]   'arrived'

(194) /e/ → [ɛ] / __ $\begin{bmatrix} +\text{nas} \\ +\text{ant} \end{bmatrix}$ \$

[ɛ] occurs following vowels word finally as shown in (195) This leads to the rule shown in (196).

(195) [hɔ⁵³.ɛ²¹] 'plant'

(196) /e/ → [ɛ] / V\$ __ #

This is a result of utterance-final vowel lowering due to lack of stress on verbal suffixes. [e] does not occur in these environments.

The vowel [ɛ] occurs in free variation with [e] following syllable-final glottal stop and glides (diphthongs ending in /u i/). Note the examples shown in (197). This leads to the rule shown in (198).

(197) [jɔʔ³².e³] ~ [jɔʔ³².ɛ³] 'lick'   [ʃai³¹.ɛ²] ~ [ʃai³¹.e²] 'different'

(198) /e/ → [e] ~ [ɛ] / \$ __ #

The vowel [e] occurs in free variation with [ɛ] following syllable-final plosives and nasals, except in the case where the vowel preceding the final is [−low] and [−ATR], as in [ɪ ɛ ʊ]. In this case the [−ATR] feature spreads to the word-final vowel, making it [ɛ] in all cases. This is a form of limited vowel harmony.[115] In cases where the [−low vowel] preceding the final plosive is still [+ATR] due to a preceding palatal, the lowering effect on the final verb particle is still observed. This shows that two independent processes are involved. The first is the lowering of a [+ATR] vowel to a [−ATR] vowel in a checked syllable, and the second is the raising of the [−ATR] vowel following a palatal consonant. The

---

[115]This process does not occur with vowels in stressed syllables following syllables with [−ATR] vowels, e.g., [mʊt⁴.dum⁵³] 'cloud', [sɪk⁵.ʃi³¹] 'fruit'.

vowel harmony follows word-internal vowel lowering and precedes vowel raising of the verbal suffix as shown in (199).[116] Examples are given in (200) which leads to the rule shown in (201).

(199)   checked syllable   vowel harmony   vowel raising
                 vowel lowering
     /pʰjik.e/ 'spicy' ⟶ pʰjɪk.e ⟶ pʰjɪk.ɛ ⟶ pʰjik.ɛ

(200) [tʃʰɔ⁵³m.e³¹] ~ [tʃʰɔ⁵³m.ɛ³¹] 'help each other'   [pʰji⁵k.ɛ²¹] 'spicy'
       [wa³¹p.e²] ~ [wa³¹p.ɛ²] 'bark'   [mɪ³t.ɛ³] 'think'
       [sʊ³p.ɛ³] 'play'   [kjɪ⁴²n.ɛ²³] 'scratch'
       [dɪ³²n.ɛ²¹] 'run'   [kʰju⁵⁴p.ɛ²¹] 'sew'

(201) /e/ → [ɛ] / V   [+cons] $ __ #
              [−ATR]
      [e] ~ [ɛ] / word finally elsewhere

This process is only observed with the suffix /ʔe/ since it is the only unstressed suffix occurring phonetically as a V syllable type.[117] The suffixes /be/ (completive action) and /le/ (imperfective) do not undergo similar allophonic variation.

The vowel /e/ has an [ɛ] offglide, [eᵋ], following a syllable-initial consonant word finally as shown in (202). This leads to the diphthongization rule shown in (203).

(202) [wu⁵³ŋ.beᵋ³²] 'wild cats'   [ʔa².seᵋ³] 'not know'

(203) /e/ → [eᵋ] / $C__#

[e] does not occur in this environment.

The vowel [ʊ] is an allophone of /u/. [ʊ] occurs in syllables checked by /t/ and /k/ when not preceded by alveopalatal affricates or [j], but not in syllables checked by /ʔ/ and /p/, as shown in (204) which leads to the rule shown in (205).

(204) [sʊ⁵⁴.ɛ²¹] 'wipe'   [dʑut⁵.ɛ²] 'slippery'
       [mʊt⁴.dum⁵³] 'cloud'   [mjuk⁵⁴.e²¹] 'bury'
       [ʃʊt⁵⁴.ɛ³²] 'wrong'   [ʃuʔ⁵.ɛ²] 'drink'
       [bʊt³².ɛ³] 'rotton'   [bup³.ɛ³] 'rotton'

---

[116] Only vowel processes are shown for simplification.
[117] For a discussion of glottal stop elision pertaining to /ʔe/ (perfective), see § A.7.

Appendix A

(205)
$$/u/ \rightarrow [\upsilon] \ / \ \text{not} \begin{Bmatrix} [\text{aff}] \\ [j] \end{Bmatrix} \_\_ \begin{Bmatrix} \begin{bmatrix} -\text{son} \\ +\text{ant} \end{bmatrix} \\ \begin{bmatrix} -\text{son} \\ +\text{bk} \end{bmatrix} \end{Bmatrix} \$$$

[u] does not occur in these environments. The exclusion of /p/ in addition to /ʔ/ as an environment for lowering /u/ may be due to the larger oral cavity inherent with /p/ and thus a longer articulation or transition period for the preceding vowel as discussed in §6.3.1. The alveopalatal affricates and the glide /j/, preceding the back vowel, prevent [−ATR] due to their [+hi], [−bk] features, which correlate with [+ATR].

In syllables closed by a [cor], [ʊ] occurs following glottal stops as shown in (206) which leads to the rule shown in (207).

(206) [ʔʊt⁵.ʤam³¹] 'water'   [ʔu³².kʰuʔ⁵⁴] 'pillow'
      [mə³.ʔʊn⁵³.si³¹] 'coconut'   [ʔʊŋ⁵³.ɛ³²] 'sell'

(207) /u/ → [ʊ] /ʔ/ __ C$
                        [cor]

[ʊ] is in free variation with [u] in checked syllables when preceded by a /w/ as shown in (208) which leads to the rule shown in (209).

(208) [wʊt².ɛ³] ~ [wut².ɛ³]   'call to'
      [dzan³².wʊt⁵] ~ [dzan³².wut⁵] 'year'

(209) /u/ → [ʊ] ~ [u] / /w/ __C$
                          $\begin{bmatrix} -\text{cont} \\ -\text{son} \end{bmatrix}$

Vowel reduction

The vowel [ə] occurs as the only vowel in word-initial, reduced syllables which were derived from historical CC clusters which underwent vowel epenthesis. Vowels other than [ə] never occur in these types of reduced syllables. It is not possible synchronically to determine from which vowel the [ə] originates in the nonproductive reduced syllables. Therefore, vowel contrast is neutralized. See the last row of (85).

There are also word-initial CV reduced syllables which are productive and normal compounded CV syllables in unstressed position. These word-initial CV syllables can carry independent meaning and contrastive tone as shown in the fourth and fifth rows of (85). Both of these prefixes can appear with vowels reduced to a [ə] in free variation with [a], but vowel contrast is not neutralized as in the presyllables.

Additional processes

There are three allophonic processes which are very rare due to the specific environments required. They will be briefly mentioned here.

The vowel [æ] precedes a labial consonant while [e] or [ɛ] never do. Therefore, [æ] is an allophone of /e/. Note the examples shown in (210).

(210) [nɔ³.kʰjæp⁵] 'ear' [lap̰⁴.pʰjet⁵⁴.e¹] 'lightning'
     [kʰjæm⁵³.gi³] 'space under house' [ja³².pʰjɛn³] 'opium'

The vowel [ɨ] occurs following [p], [pʰ], and [b] and preceding [k] while [a i u] never do. This seeming allophonic variation is very similar to what Matisoff (1973a:3) calls "dissimilation of lip action that is difficult to capture in present versions of distinctive-feature terminology." Matisoff theorizes that the change of the Black Lahu /u/ to [ɯ] following bilabials is due to the /u/ losing its roundedness feature to the bilabials preceding it. Therefore, it is most probable that [ɨ] is an allophone of /u/. If this is the case the vowel loses roundness and is fronted. Note the examples shown in (211).

(211) [bɨk³².e³] 'shoot'
     [pɨk⁵⁴.e²¹] 'kick'
     [lə³.kɔ⁴³ʔ.pʰɨ⁵⁴k.e²¹] 'catch fish'

The vowel [ɯ] occurs following [h] and preceding [ŋ] while [u] never does. The vowel loses its roundness. Note the examples shown in (212).

(212) [hɯ⁵³ŋ] 'gold' [hu³.sʊn⁵⁴.pʰju⁵¹] 'garlic'
     [hɯŋ⁴³.ɛ³] 'long' [lə³.hiŋ³⁵.juʔ⁵³] 'thousand people'

Appendix A

A.5 Additional discussion on the distribution of phonemes

The consonant/modal vowel combinations with simple and complex onsets are shown in (213).

(213)

	/i/	/e/	/a/	/u/	/ɔ/	/au/	/ai/	/ui/	/ɔi/
/pʰ/	x	x	x	x	x	x		x	x
/pʰj/	x	x	x	x	x			x	x
/b/	x	x	x	x	x	x		x	x
/bj/	x	x	x	x	x				
/tʰ/	x	x	x	x	x	x	x	x	
/d/	x	x	x	x	x	x	x	x	
/kʰ/	x	x	x	x	x	x	x	x	x
/kʰj/	x		x	x	x			x	
/kʰɹ/	x			x					
/g/	x	x	x	x	x	x	x	x	
/gj/				x	x			x	
/gɹ/							x		
/ʔ/	x	x	x	x	x				
/tsʰ/	x	x	x	x	x	x	x		
/dz/	x	x	x	x	x	x	x	x	x
/tʃʰ/	x	x	x	x	x				x
/dʒ/	x	x	x	x	x				
/s/	x	x	x	x	x	x	x	x	x
/ʃ/	x	x	x	x	x	x	x	x	x
/m/	x	x	x	x	x	x	x	x	x
/mj/	x		x	x	x				x
/n/	x	x	x	x	x	x	x		
/nj/	x	x	x		x				
/ŋ/			x	x	x	x			
/l/	x	x	x	x	x	x	x	x	x
/ɹ/			x	x					
/w/	x	x	x	x	x	x		x	x
/j/		x	x	x	x			x	
/h/	x	x	x	x	x	x	x	x	x

Some gaps in consonant/vowel combinations are likely due to the low incidence of the vowels /e ɔi/ and the consonant /ɹ/. There are several gaps in the table which are most likely not due to a lack of data. Front vowels do not follow /ŋ/. This corresponds to a gap in *velar + *front vowels in the proto-language (Bradley 1979:119). The high, front vowel does not follow syllable initial /j/. The absence of /i/ following syllable initial /j/ may be due to dissimilation. It is interesting to note that /i/

generally follows /nj/ and only in one syllable does /i/ follow /n/, /nik/. There may be a process of $n \rightarrow nj \:/ \_\_ i$ taking place which also occurs in Lahu (Matisoff 1973a:5). The only diphthong that follows the /j/ and alveopalatal affricates is /ui/.[118] If the palatal affricates are interpreted as alveolar plosives followed by /j/, then the distribution is generalized to following /j/. /n/ and /ŋ/ do not precede /ui/ or /ai/. Bilabial plosives do not precede /ai/.

The observed initial consonant/tense vowel combinations are shown in (214)

(214)

	/i̤/	/ɛ̤/	/a̤/	/ṳ/	/ɔ̤/	/a̤u/	/a̤i/	/ṳi/	/ɔ̤i/
/pʰ/									
/b/	x		x	x	x				
/bj/									
/tʰ/									
/d/	x	x	x		x	x	x	x	
/kʰ/									
/kʰj/									
/g/			x	x	x				
/gj/	x		x	x	x				
/gɹ/									
/ʔ/	x		x	x		x			
/tsʰ/									
/dz/				x					
/tʃʰ/									
/ʤ/	x		x	x	x				x
/s/									
/ʃ/									
/m/	x			x	x				
/mj/	x		x	x	x				
/n/	x		x	x	v				
/nj/	x	x	x						
/ŋ/			x	x	x				
/l/			x	x	x			x	
/ɹ/	x								
/w/	x		x						
/j/			x	x	x				
/h/									

---

[118]The only exception to this is the single occurrence of /ɔ̤i/ following /ʤ/. A further generalization can then be made stating that only diphthongs with palatal offglides follow /j/.

Appendix A

Many gaps are due to a lack of tense voice syllables in the data. Gaps which may be significant are: front, tense vowels do not follow /ŋ/ or syllable initial /j/, tense vowels do not follow [+spread vf] initials as noted in §5.5.

The VC combinations which make up the syllable rhyme present four interesting holes and patterns in co-occurence: (1) /i/ does not precede labial consonants; (2) /i/ very rarely precedes /ʔ/; (3) /u ɔ/ precede /ʔ/ a high percentage of the time; and (4) /ạ/ does not precede /k/, and /ak/ is very rare.

The explanation for a lack of /ak/ and /ạk/ is most likely historical, paralleling the same process from Burmese. Lehman (1991:3) explains the reason why written Burmese spells words with an -ak which are now phonetically [et]: "the apparent shift of the consonant from velar to apical appears to be part of an old phonological tendency of the language, a long-term trend towards a binary contrastive distribution between velar and dental syllable finals: dentals following simplex vowels, velars following diphthongs/glides." The motivation for the other holes in co-occurence is unknown. They may be due to historical gaps or accidental gaps.

Consonant/nasal (... VC$_3$.NV ...) clusters across syllable boundaries have the limitations shown in (215).

(215)   Syl 2 onset

Syl 1 coda	m	n	ŋ
bilabial	x		
alveolar	x	x	
velar	x	x	
glottal	x	x	

The velar nasal only occurs word initially or syllable finally and never occurs syllable initially internal to a word.[119] A bilabial coda only precedes a bilabial nasal of syllable 2. Further study needs to be done in this area to identify any morphophonemic processes contributing to limitations in co-occurrence.

An interesting gap occurs between C_i and C_f. Syllables with a labial or velar nasal C_i do not have labial or velar finals, respectively, as shown in (216).

(216)   *mVC   *ŋVC
         [lab]   [high]

---

[119]The one exception is the negative prefix /a²/ preceding an affirmative /ŋʊt/ to give [a².ŋʊt⁴] 'no'.

This may be an interesting topic for a study in word formation, but the scope is beyond this analysis.

A.6 Allophone statements

Zaiwa consonant phonemes

All sounds are made with pulmonic egressive air.

/pʰ/	[pʰ]	voiceless aspirated bilabial plosive. Never with tense syllables. /pʰjɔ⁵³/ [pʰjɔ⁵³] 'cockroach'
/b/	[b]	voiced bilabial plosive. Only slightly voiced, never with tense syllables. /bui³¹/ [bui³¹] 'sun'
	[p]	voiceless unaspirated bilabial plosive. Only with tense syllables. /bja̰ŋ⁵³e⁴/ [pja̰ŋ⁵³ɛ²¹] 'winnow'
	[pʔ]	voiceless unaspirated bilabial plosive co-articulated with glottal stop. Syllable finally only. /hub/ [hʊp⁷⁵] 'small leech'
/tʰ/	[tʰ]	voiceless aspirated alveolar plosive. Never with tense syllables. /tʰaŋ³¹/ [tʰaŋ³¹] 'firewood'
/d/	[d]	voiced alveolar plosive. Only slightly voiced, never with tense syllables. /duŋ³¹/ [duŋ³¹] 'wing'
	[t]	voiceless unaspirated alveolar plosive. Only with tense syllables. /da̰u³¹e⁴/ [ta̰u³¹.ɛ¹²] 'answer'
	[tʔ]	voiceless unaspirated alveolar plosive co-articulated with glottal stop. Syllable finally only. /nṵd/ [nṵt⁷⁵] 'mouth'
/kʰ/	[kʰ]	voiceless aspirated velar plosive. Never with tense syllables. /kʰui³¹/ [kʰui³¹] 'dog'
/g/	[g]	voiced velar plosive. Only slightly voiced, never with tense syllables. /guʔ³²/ [guʔ³²] 'paddy rice'
	[k]	voiceless unaspirated velar plosive. Only with tense syllables. /gɔ̰⁵³e⁴/ [kɔ̰⁵³.ɛ²] 'big'
	[kʔ]	voiceless unaspirated velar plosive co-articulated with glottal stop. Syllable finally only. /nik/ [nɪkʔ³²] 'bamboo shoot'
/ʔ/	[ʔ]	glottal plosive. Only contrastive word finally. /ʔi⁵³.pʰe⁵³/ [ʔi⁵pʰe⁵¹] 'liquor'
/tsʰ/	[tsʰ]	voiceless aspirated alveolar affricate. Never with tense syllables. /tsʰɔ³¹/ [tsʰɔ³¹] 'salt'
/dz/	[dz]	voiced alveolar affricate. /dzaŋ³¹/ [dzaŋ³¹] 'cooked rice'
	[ts]	voiceless alveolar affricate. Only with tense syllables. /dzṵŋ⁵³e⁴/ [tsṵŋ⁵³.ɛ²¹] 'same'
/tʃʰ/	[tʃʰ]	voiceless aspirated alveopalatal grooved affricate. Never with tense syllables. /tʃʰɔ³¹/ [tʃʰɔ³¹] 'hive'

/dʑ/	[dʑ]	voiced alveopalatal grooved affricate. Occurs with both tense and modal syllables. /dʑape⁴/ [dʑa̱b⁵⁴.e³] 'narrow'
	[tsʃ]	voiceless unaspirated alveopalatal grooved affricate. Only with tense syllables. /ga³¹.dʑɔg/ [gə³².tʃɔk⁵⁴] 'armpit'
/s/	[s]	voiceless alveolar grooved fricative. /siŋ³¹/ [siŋ⁴²] 'liver'
/ʃ/	[ʃ]	voiceless alveopalatal grooved fricative. /ʃi⁴dʑi⁴/ [ʃɪ⁴.dʑi⁴] 'seed'
/h/	[h]	voiceless glottal fricative. (more friction than English [h]) /huŋ⁵³/ [hu̱ŋ⁵³] 'gold'
/m/	[m]	voiced bilabial nasal. /mau³¹/ [mau³¹] 'rain'
/n/	[n]	voiced alveolar nasal. /nɔ⁴nau⁴/ [nɔ³.nau³] 'milk'
/ŋ/	[ŋ]	voiced velar nasal. /ŋɔ³¹/ [ŋɔ³¹] 1st person singular pronoun
/l/	[l]	voiced alveolar lateral. /le⁴e⁴/ [le³.ɛ³] 'come'
/ɹ/	[ɹ]	voiced indeterminate retroflexed nonsyllabic vocoid. (some friction) /ɹa⁴e⁴/ [ɹa³.ɛ³²] 'smooth'
/j/	[j]	voiced palatal central approximant. /jɔʔe⁴/ [jɔʔ³².e³] 'lick'
/w/[120]	[w]	voiced labiovelar approximant. w precedes /i e au ai/, [w] is in free variation with [βʷ] preceding /ɔ/, [w] is in free variation with [βʷ] and [v] preceding /a/. /wi³¹laŋ³¹/ [wi³.laŋ³¹] 'river'
	[v]	voiced labiodental fricative. Very little labiodental friction present. [v] precedes /u/, [v] is in free variation with w and [βʷ] preceding /a/. /wum⁴bɔ³¹e⁴/ [vum⁴³.bɔ²¹.ɛ²] 'strong'
	[βʷ]	voiced bilabial fricative with labialized offglide. [βʷ] is in free variation with [w] preceding /ɔ/ and in free variation with [w] and [v] preceding /a/. /wɔʔ/ [βʷɔʔ³²] ~ [wɔʔ³²] 'chicken'

Zaiwa vowel phonemes

Simple vowels

/i/	[i]	voiced high close front unrounded vocoid. /dziŋ³¹/ [dziŋ³¹] 'drum'
	[ɪ]	voiced high open front unrounded vocoid. In checked syllables in which C_1 or C_2 is not /j/, in open syllables with C_1 an alveopalatal and C_1 of the following syllable a [−cont] obstruent, and in syllables closed by an /n/. /mide⁴/ [mɪt³.ɛ³] 'think'

---

[120]Allophonic variation for /w/ is speaker dependent. The description here is from speaker 1, §A.2.

/e/	[e]	voiced mid close front unrounded vocoid. /be^{53}e/ [be^{53}.ɛ^{31}] 'already'
	[ɛ]	voiced mid open front unrounded vocoid. In syllables followed by a [−cont] obstruent, in syllables in which C_1 or C_2 is /j/, following vowels word finally, and in syllables closed with an /n/. In free variation with [e] following syllable final plosives, nasals, and glides. /dʒen^{53}e^4/ [dʒen^{53}.ɛ^{31}] 'filter'
	[eᶜ]	voiced mid close front unrounded vocoid with open offglide. Following a consonant word finally. /se^4/ [seᵋ^4] know
	[æ]	voiced low close front unrounded vocoid. In syllables in which C_3 is labial. /kʰjem^{53}gi^4/ [kʰjæm^{53}.gi^3] 'space under house'
/a/	[a]	voiced low open central unrounded vocoid. /tʰaŋ^{31}/ [tʰaŋ^{31}] 'firewood'
/u/	[u]	voiced high close back rounded vocoid. Tends to be lowered toward [o] preceding [+back] consonants. /bum^{31}/ [bum^{31}] 'mountain'
	[ʊ]	voiced high open back rounded vocoid. In syllables checked by /t k/ with C_1 not an alveopalatal affricate or [j], or following a /ʔ/ in syllables closed by an /n/. /mude^4/ [mʊt^{32}.ɛ^3] 'hungry'
	[ɨ]	voiced high close central unrounded vocoid. In checked syllables with C_1 a labial and C_3 [+high]. /buge^4/ [bɨk^3.e^3] 'shoot'
/ɔ/	[ɔ]	voiced low close back rounded vocoid. Tends to be raised following [+high] (alveopalatal and velar) consonants. /bjɔ^{31}/ [bjɔ^{31}] 'bee'
	[ə]	voiced mid close central unrounded vocoid. In free variation with [a u i ɔ] in word-initial, open syllables. Also the only vowel present in reduced syllables. /la^{31}mɔ^4/ [lə^{32}.mɔ^2] ~ [la^{32}.mɔ^2] 'tiger'

Diphthongs

/ai/	[ai]	voiced low open central unrounded vocoid with high close front unrounded offglide. /lai^{53}e^4/ [lai^{53}.ɛ^{32}] heavy
/au/	[au]	voiced low open central unrounded vocoid with high close back rounded offglide. /tʰau^{53}e^4/ [tʰau^{52}.e^{21}] stab
/ui/	[ui]	voiced high close back rounded vocoid with high close front unrounded offglide. /dzui^{31}/ [dzui^{31}] tooth
/ɔi/	[ɔi]	voiced low back rounded vocoid with high close front unrounded offglide. /lahɔi^4/ [la^3.hɔi^4] snail

Appendix A   145

A.7 Morphophonemics

Coronal consonant epenthesis

The plosive [t] is epenthesized, closing a word-initial CV syllable, where V is /u ɔ a/,[121] and the initial consonant of the following syllable is a coronal. This process has some dependency on stress, but the details have not been worked out. Note the examples shown in (217).[122]

(217) a. [nɔt³.lui³¹]   /nɔ³¹lui³¹/   'buffalo' [nɔ³¹]   'cow or buffalo'
      b. [ʔʊt³².lum³¹] /ʔu³¹lum³¹/   'head'   [ʔu³.kʰuʔ⁵⁴]   'pillow'
      c. [kʰət⁴³.nạm³²] /kʰa⁴.nạm³¹/ 'when'   [kʰa⁴³.juʔ³²] 'who'

Epenthesis is indicated rather than deletion due to the open syllable structure of the affected syllables in isolation, as in (217a). The occurrence of unaffected syllables checked by a [t] when not in the indicated environment for epenthesis further verifies the process, e.g., compare [ʔʊt⁵] 'gong' with (217b).

Coronal epenthesis is represented by the rule shown in (218).

(218) ∅ → [t] / C V __ $ C
               [+bk]   cor
                         |
                       [+ant]

This process can be represented in an autosegmental framework by inserting an unmarked consonant and spreading place from the following consonant as shown in (219).

(219)
        ↓
    C V   C   C
    | ⸱⸱⸱⸱⸱|
    dor   cor
    | |
   [+bk]   [+ant]

---

[121][ə] in example (217) is an allophone of /a/ in an unstressed syllable.

[122]The process of checked syllable tone derivation discussed in §4.4 must precede the morphophonemic coronal consonant epenthesis due to the fact that the examples [ʔʊt³².lum³¹] 'head' and [kʰət⁴³.nạm³²] 'when', do not carry a high tone.

Place assimilation

The syllable final /ʔ/ can assimilate to labial and velar place before a labial or velar consonant, respectively. The process is not observed in all data and generally occurs in normal to fast speech. The syllable-final /ʔ/ can be heard in slow speech or when the syllable is in isolation. Note the examples shown in (220) which leads to the rules shown in (221).

(220) [wap³².ma⁴²] ~ [waʔ³².ma⁴²]   /waʔma⁴/   'carry on shoulder'

[mjɔp³².mau³] ~ [mjɔʔ³².mau³]   /mjɔʔmau⁴/   'eyebrow'

[suk⁵.kan³¹.be³².ɛ²] ~   /suʔkan³¹be⁴e⁴/   'spit'
[suʔ⁵.kan³¹.be³².ɛ²]

(221) [ʔ] ~ [p]/ __ $C
                    [+lab]

[ʔ] ~ [k]/ __ $C
                 [+bk]

This process can be represented in an autosegmental framework by assuming that the glottal stop has a laryngeal place node associated with [+const vf] and an empty oral place node as shown in (222). The oral place of the following consonant can spread to the empty oral place node producing a co-articulated stop/glottal stop, which is identical to the structure of all other syllable-final stops in Zaiwa.

(222)   [ʔ]   [p k]
            ╱   ╲ |
        glot   oral   oral
          | ╲------┘
     [+const vf]   ⎰lab⎱
                     ⎱dor⎰

It is not clear why this process is not productive with /t/ as the following consonant.

Glottal elision

A syllable-initial glottal stop is deleted following a consonant word internally and between a word and a conjunction.[123] Note the examples shown in (223) which lead to the rule shown in (224).

(223) [dzuŋ³².aʔ²¹]   /dzuŋ³²ʔaʔ/   'sit down (imperative)'
       [jaŋ³².ɛʔ¹²]   /jaŋ³¹ʔeʔ/   'with him'
       [tʃʉn⁵.am⁴³.e²¹]   /dʒʉn⁵³ʔam⁴e⁴/   'push into'

(224) ʔ → ∅ / C $__

In fast speech, the vowel-initial syllable created by glottal elision may be pronounced with an initial nasal identical to the nasal final of the preceding syllable. In this case, the words in (223) are pronounced as shown in (225).

(225) [dzuŋ³².ŋaʔ²¹]   'sit down (imperative)'
       [jaŋ³².ŋɛʔ¹²]   'with him'
       [tʃʉn⁵.nam⁴³.me²¹]   'push into'

(226) ʔ → ∅ / V $__ in unstressed syllable #

The syllable-initial glottal stop in a stressed syllable is pronounced following a final vowel of the preceding syllable, e.g., [ʔa³.ʔɔ³¹] downstream.

Voicing assimilation

Syllable-final [k] tends to become voiced to [g] preceding a voiced consonant if neither syllable is tense. The stiff vocal folds of tense voice tend to repress voicing, even across syllable boundaries. Note the examples shown in (227).

---

[123]Matisoff (1989b:165) addresses case and aspect particles by saying, "since these functors... are naturally unstressed by comparison with their preceding root-word, they are prime candidates for sloppy articulation and phonological reduction", and in reference to Lahu, "postpositional particles are apt to lose their initial consonant in rapid speech" Glottal elision occurs in Lahu. Matisoff (1973:10) concludes from this elision that "[ʔ] thus has no phonemic status at all in syllable-initial position." In syllable-final position Matisoff considers [ʔ] to be a feature of the tone. This differs from Zaiwa in that in Lahu, there is no syllable-final contrast between the glottal stop and its absence, while in Zaiwa there is contrast.

(227) [sɪg⁵.gam⁵³]   /siggam⁵³/   'tree'
      [sɪg⁵⁴.mɪt⁴³]   /sigmit/   'root'
      [nɪ̠k⁵.lum³¹]   /nɪ̠glum³¹/   'heart'
      [ʃɪ³.pʰjik⁵.ne̠ᶜ⁵³.ʃi³¹] /ʃi³¹pʰjigne⁵³ʃi³¹/ 'red pepper'

This leads to the rule shown in (228).

(228) /g/ → [+slack vf] / _ $ C
                              [+slack vf]

Note that an obstruent with slack vocal folds is voiced as shown in rule (57), §4.4.3. This process can be shown autosegmentally. The [k] is underlyingly associated with the feature [+const vf]. When followed by a voiced consonant, the [+const vf] feature is deleted, and the glottal feature from the following consonant spreads to the empty node as shown in (229).

(229)

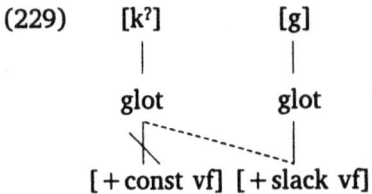

In a tense syllable, the feature [+stiff vf] is also associated with the /k/. When the [+const vf] feature is deleted, the [+stiff vf] feature is still present to give a voiceless consonant according to rule (57). Since stiff and slack vocal folds cannot co-occur, the [+slack vf] feature cannot spread. This is shown in (230).

(230)

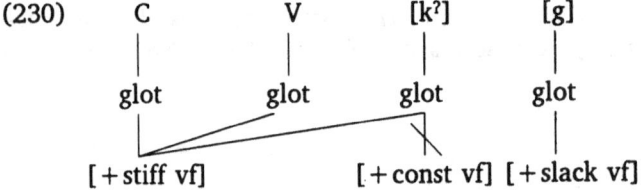

It is unclear why this occurs with [k] only.

Appendix B
Distinctive Feature Charts

(231) Zaiwa consonant distinctive features

Place	Feature	pʰ	p	b	tʰ	t	d	kʰ	k	g	tsʰ	ts	dz
Root	sonorant	−	−	−	−	−	−	−	−	−	−	−	−
	cons	+	+	+	+	+	+	+	+	+	+	+	+
	cont	−	−	−	−	−	−	−	−	−	−/+	−/+	−/+
	strident	−	−	−	−	−	−	−	−	−	+	+	+
	lateral	−	−	−	−	−	−	−	−	−	−	−	−
Coronal	anterior				+	+	+				+	+	+
	distrib				−	−	−				−	−	−
Soft palate	nasal	−	−	−	−	−	−	−	−	−	−	−	−
Dorsal	high							+	+	+			
	back							+	+	+			
Labial	round	−	−	−									
Laryngeal	voice	−	−	+	−	−	+	−	−	+	−	−	+
	stiff vf	+	+	−	+	+	−	+	+	−	+	+	−
	spread vf	+	−	−	+	−	−	+	−	−	+	−	−
	const vf	−	−	−	−	−	−	−	−	−	−	−	−

Appendix B

Place	Feature	m	n	ŋ	tʃʰ	tʃ	dʒ	ßʷ	v	s	ʃ
Root	sonorant	+	+	+	−	−	−	−	−	−	−
	cons	+	+	+	+	+	+	+	+	+	+
	cont	−	−	−	−/+	−/+	−/+	+	+	+	+
	strident	−	−	−	+	+	+	+	+	+	+
	lateral	−	−	−	−	−	−	−	−	−	−
Coronal	anterior	+	+		+	+	+		+	+	+
	distrib	−	−		−	−	−		−	−	−
Soft palate	nasal	+	+	+	−	−	−	−	−	−	−
Dorsal	high			+	+	+	+				
	back			+	−	−	−				
Labial	round	−						+	−		
Laryngeal	voice	+	+	+	−	−	+	+	+	−	−
	stiff vf	−	−	−	+	+	−	−	−	−	−
	spread vf	−	−	−	+	−	−	−	−	−	−
	const vf	−	−	−	−	−	−	−	−	−	−

Aspects of Zaiwa Prosody

Place	Feature	ɹ	l	j	w	ʔ	pʔ	tʔ	kʔ	h
Root	sonorant	+	+	+	+	−	−	−	−	−
	cons	+	+	+	+	+	+	+	+	+
	cont	+	+	+	+	−	−	−	−	+
	strident	−	−	−	−	−	−	−	−	−
	lateral	−	+	−	−	−	−	−	−	−
Coronal	anterior	+	+		+		+	+		
	distrib	−	−	+	−		−	−		
Soft palate	nasal	−	−	−	−	−			−	−
Dorsal	high			+	+	−			+	−
	back			−	+	−			+	−
Labial	round				+	−	−			
Laryngeal	voice	+	+	+	+	−	−	−	−	−
	stiff vf	−	−	−	−	−	−	−	−	−
	spread vf	−	−	−	−	−	−	−	−	+
	const vf	−	−	−	−	+	+	+	+	−

Appendix B

(232) Zaiwa vowel distinctive features

Place	Feature	i	ɪ	e	ɛ	æ	ɨ	ə	a	ɯ	u	ʊ	ɔ
Root	sonorant	+	+	+	+	+	+	+	+	+	+	+	+
	consonant	−	−	−	−	−	−	−	−	−	−	−	−
Soft palate	nasal	−	−	−	−	−	−	−	−	−	−	−	−
Dorsal	high	+	+	−	−	−	+	−	−	+	+	+	−
	low	−	−	−	−	+	−	−	+	−	−	−	+
	back	−	−	−	−	−	+	+	+	+	+	+	+
Labial	round	−	−	−	−	−	−	−	−	−	+	+	+
Laryngeal	voice	+	+	+	+	+	+	+	+	+	+	+	+
	stiff vf	−	−	−	−	−	−	−	−	−	−	−	−
	spread vf	−	−	−	−	−	−	−	−	−	−	−	−
	cons vf	−	−	−	−	−	−	−	−	−	−	−	−
Tongue root	ATR	+	−	+	−	+	+	+	−	+	+	−	+

(233) Zaiwa suprasegmental distinctive features

Place	Feature	V⁵	V³	tense vq
Laryngeal	voice			
	stiff vf	+	−	+
	spread vf	+		
	const vf	+ +	+/−	

References

Anderson, Stephen R. 1978. Tone features. In Victoria A. Fromkin (ed.), Tone: A linguistic survey, 133–76. New York: Academic Press.
———. 1979.
Bao, Zhiming. 1990. On the nature of tone. Ph.D. dissertation. Massachusetts Institute of Technology.
Benedict, Paul K. 1948. Tonal systems in Southeast Asia. Journal of the American Oriental Society 68(4):184–91.
———. 1972. Sino-Tibetan: A conspectus. Princeton-Cambridge studies in Chinese linguistics 2. Cambridge: Cambridge University Press.
Bradley, David. 1971. Prefixes and suffixes in Tibeto-Burman and Burmese-Lolo. Fourth Sino-Tibetan Conference Papers. Bloomington: Indiana University.
———. 1977. Proto-Loloish tones. Pacific Linguistics Series A, 49:1–22. Papers in Southeast Asian linguistics 5. Canberra: Department of Linguistics, Research School of the Pacific Studies, The Australian National University.
———. 1979. Proto-Loloish. Scandinavian Institute of Asian Studies monograph series 39. London: Curzon Press.
———. 1982. Register in Burmese. Pacific Linguistics, Series A, 62.
———. 1993. Pronouns in Burmese-Lolo. Linguistics of the Tibeto-Burman Area 16(1):157–215.
Burling, Robbins. 1966. The addition of final stops in the history of Maru. Language 42(3):581–86.

———. 1967. Proto-Lolo Burmese. International Journal of American Linguistics 33(2):part 2. Bloomington: Indiana University.
Chao, Yuan-ren. 1930. A system of tone letters. Maitre Phonetique 30:24–27.
———. 1968. A grammar of spoken Chinese. Berkeley: University of California Press.
Chelliah, Shobhana L. 1991. Tone in Manipuri. Austin: University of Texas at Austin.
Cheng Mo. 1956. Zaiwa-yu Jianjie (A brief introduction of the Atsi language). Zhongguo Yuwen (Chinese Language) 53:41–44. Beijing.
Clements, G. N. 1985. The geometry of phonological features. Phonology Yearbook 2:225–52.
Cornyn, William Stewart. 1944. Outline of Burmese grammar. Language 20(4):Supplement.
Dai Qingxia. 1986. Zaiwa-yu (The Atsi language). Zhongguo Dabaike Quanshu: Minzu. (Magna Encyclopedia Sinica: Ethnology Volume).
———. 1993. A genetic classification for Tibeto-Burman languages in China. In Recent contributions to Tibeto-Burman studies. Beijing: CUN Press.
Dai Qingxia and Yan Mu Chu. 1990. The tones of Zaiwa. Research on Tibeto-Burman languages, 351–68. Kunming: Yunnan Nationalities Publishing House.
Diehl, Lon. 1992a. The Kachin in China: Who calls whom what. Unpublished manuscript.
———. 1992b. The personal pronouns of Jinghpo: Towards a linguistic analysis of a simple-looking paradigm. Presented at the 25th Sino-Tibetan Language Conference, Berkeley, CA.
———. 1993. Jinghpo: Negation and tone sandhi. Unpublished manuscript.
Duanmu, San. 1991. A featural analysis of some onset-vowel interactions. Proceedings of the First Annual Conference of the South East Asian Linguistics Society. Detroit: Wayne State University.
———. 1992. An autosegmental analysis of tone in four Tibetan languages. Linguistics of the Tibeto-Burman Area 15(1):65–91.
Edkins, Joseph. 1853. Colloquial Chinese as exhibited in the Shanghai dialect. Shanghai: Presbyterian Mission Press.
Edmondson, Jerold A. 1993. Tense-lax voice quality and the Naxi language. Arlington: The University of Texas at Arlington.
———, Deji-Sezhen Geziben, and Michael Fillippini. 1995. A cross-lectal study of Tibetan tones: Analysis and representation. Arlington: The University of Texas at Arlington.
——— and Li Shaoni. 1995. Voice quality and voice quality change in the Bai language of Yunnan Province. Linguistics of the Tibeto-Burman Area 17(2).

References

Egerod, Soren. 1974. Sino-Tibetan languages. Encyclopedia Brittanica 16:796–806.

———. 1985. Typological features in Akha. In Graham Thurgood, James A. Matisoff, and David Bradley (eds.), Linguistics of the Sino-Tibetan area: The state of the art. Pacific Linguistics Series C, 87:96–104. Canberra: Department of Linguistics, Research School of the Pacific Studies, The Australian National University.

Glover, Warren W. 1971. Register in Tibeto-Burman languages of Nepal: A comparison with Mon-Khmer. In Warren Glover, Maria Hari, and E. R. Hope (eds.), Papers in South East Asian Linguistics. Pacific Linguistics Series A, 29:1–22. Canberra: The Australian National University.

Goldsmith, John A. 1976. Autosegmental phonology. Ph.D. dissertation. Bloomington: Indiana University Linguistics Club.

———. 1990. Autosegmental and metrical phonology. Oxford: Basil Blackwell.

Hale, Austin. 1982. Research on Tibeto-Burman languages. Trends in Linguistics State of the Art Report 14. New York: Mouton.

Halle, Morris. 1992. Phonological features. In William Bright (ed.), International encyclopedia of linguistics, vol. 3, 207–12.

Halle, Morris and Kenneth N. Stevens. 1971. A note on laryngeal features. Quarterly Progress Report, MIT Research Laboratory of Electronics 101:198–213.

Hanson, Ola. 1906. The Kachins: Their customs and traditions. Rangoon: American Baptist Mission Press.

Hanson. 1982.

Haudricourt, Andre-Georges. 1954. De l'origine des tons en vietnamien. Journal Asiatique 242:68–182.

Henderson, Eugenie J. A. 1952. The main features of Cambodian pronunciation. Bulletin of the School of Oriental and African Studies 12:713–25.

Hongkai, Sun. 1986. Notes on Tibeto-Burman consonant clusters. Linguistics of the Tibeto-Burman Area 9(1):1–21.

Hu Tan and Dai Qingxia. 1964. Haniyu yuanyin de songji. Zhongguo Yuwen 1.

Hyman, Larry M. 1973. The role of consonant types in natural tonal assimilations. Offprint from Consonant types and tone. Southern California Occasional Papers in Linguistics. Los Angeles: University of Southern California.

———. 1993. Register tones and tonal geometry. In Keith Snider and Harry van de Hulst (eds.), The phonology of tone: The representation of tonal register. Paris: Dordrecht.

Ladefoged, Peter. 1972. Language in Uganda. London and New York: Oxford University Press.

———. 1973. The features of the larynx. Journal of Phonetics 1(1):73–83.

———. 1989. Representing phonetic structure. UCLA Working Papers in Phonetics 73. Los Angeles: UCLA Department of Linguistics.

———. 1993. A course in phonetics. Fort Worth: Harcourt Brace Jovanovich College Publishers.

Laver, John. 1980. The phonetic description of voice quality. Cambridge: University Press.

———. 1994. Principles of phonetics. Cambridge: University Press.

Lehman, F. K. 1973. Tibeto-Burman syllable structure, tone, and the theory of phonological conspiracies. In Braj B. Kachru, Henry R. Kahane, and Renée Kahane (eds.), Issues in linguistics: Papers in honor of Henry and Renée Kahane, 515–47.

———. 1975. Wolfenden's non-pronominal a-prefix in Tibeto-Burman: Two arguments from Southern China and some proposed semantic correlates. Linguistics of the Tibeto-Burman Area 2(1):19–44.

———. 1991. Phonology of Upper Standard Burmese (Mandalay-Sagaing dialect), with particular reference to its implications for Burmese historical phonology. First Annual Meeting of the Southeast Asian Linguistic Society. Wayne State University, Detroit.

Lewis, Paul. 1968. Akha phonology. Anthropological Linguistics 10(2):8–18.

Maddieson, Ian. 1985. Phonetic cues to syllabification. In Victoria A. Fromkin (ed.), Phonetic linguistics: Essays in honor of Peter Ladefoged, 203–22. New York: Academic Press.

——— and Peter Ladefoged. 1985. "Tense" and "lax" in four minority languages of China. Journal of Phonetics 13:433–54.

Maran, LaRaw. 1971. Burmese and Jinghpo: A study of tonal linguistic processes. Occasional Papers of the Wolfenden Society on Tibeto-Burman Linguistics 4. Urbana: University of Illinois Department of Linguistics.

———. 1973. On becoming a tone language, A Tibeto-Burman model of tonogenesis. In Hyman, 97–114.

Maspero, Henri. 1912. Etude sur la phonetique historique de la eansue annamite. Les initiales. BEFEO 12.

Matisoff, James A. 1973a. The grammer of Lahu. University of California Publications in Linguistics 75. Berkeley and Los Angeles: University of California Press.

———. 1973b. Tonogenesis in Southeast Asia. Los Angeles: Linguistics Program, University of Southern California.

———. 1974. The tones of Jingphaw and Lolo-Burmese: Common origin versus independent development. Acta Linguistica Hafniensia, 15(2):153–212.

References

———. 1975. A new Lahu simplex/causative pair: "study/train". Linguistics of the Tibeto-Burman Area 2(1):151–53.

———. 1978. Variational semantics in Tibeto-Burman: The organic approach to linguistic comparison. Occasional Papers of the Wolfenden Society on Tibeto-Burman Linguistics 6. Philadelphia: Institute for the Study of Human Issues.

———. 1989a. Tone, intonation and sound symbolism in Lahu: loading the syllable canon. Linguistics of the Tibeto-Burman Area 12(2):14–163.

———. 1989b. The bulging monosyllable, or the mora the merrier: Echo-vowel adverbialization in Lahu. In Jeremy H. C. S. Davidson (ed.), South-East Asian linguistics: Essays in honour of Eugenie J. A. Henderson, 163–97. London: School of Oriental and African Studies, University of London.

Mazaudon, Martine. 1974. Notes on tones in Tibeto-Burman. Linguistics of the Tibeto-Burman Area 1(1):27–54.

———. 1976. Tibeto-Burman tonogenetics. Linguistics of the Tibeto-Burman Area 3(2).

———. 1977. Tibeto-Burman tonogenetics. Paris: Centre National de la Recherche Scientifique.

Morse, Robert H. 1962. Hierarchical levels of Rawang phonology. Bloomington: Department of Linguistics, Indiana University.

———. 1988. A short update on Rawang phonology. Linguistics of the Tibeto-Burman Area 11(2):120–32.

Ohala, John. 1973. The physiology of tone. In Hyman, 1–14.

Okell, John. 1979. Notes on tone alteration in Maru verbs. Twelfth International Conference on Sino-Tibetan Languages and Linguistics. Paris.

Pike, Kenneth L. 1948. Tone languages: A technique for determining the number and type of pitch contrasts in a language, with studies in tonemic substitution and fusion. Ann Arbor: University of Michigan Publications in Linguistics.

Pulleyblank, Douglas George. 1983. Tone in lexical phonology. Ph.D. dissertation, MIT.

———. 1986. Underspecification and low vowel harmony in Okpe. Studies in African Linguistics 17(2):11–151.

Schuh, Russel G. 1978. Tone rules. In Victoria A. Fromkin (ed.), Tone: A linguistic survey, 221–57. New York: Academic Press.

Shafer. 1966. Introduction to Sino-Tibetan. Wiesbaden: Harrassowitz.

Steinthal, Heymann. 1855. Zur vergleichenden Erforschung der Chinesischen Sprache. To appear in J. Leopold (ed.), Prix Volnay. Dordrecht: Kluwer.

Wang, William. 1967. The phonological features of tone. International Journal of American Linguistics 33:93–105.

Weidert, Alfons. 1979. The Sino-Tibetan tonogenetic laryngeal reconstruction theory. Linguistics of the Tibeto-Burman Area 5(1):49–127.

Wolfenden, Stuart. 1929. Outlines of Tibeto-Burman linguistic morphology. Royal Asiatic Society Prize Publication 12. London: Royal Asiatic Society.

Xu Xijian and Xu Guizhen. 1984. Jingpo-zu Yuyan Jianzhi (Zaiwa-yu). (Outline of the Zaiwa language of the Kachin nationality). Outline of China's Minority Language Series. Beijing: Nationalities Publishing House.

Yabu, Shiro. 1988. A preliminary report on the study of the Maru, Lashi and Atsi languages of Burma. In Yoshiaki Ishizawa (ed.), Historical and cultural studies in Burma, 65–132. Tokyo: Institute of Asian Studies, Sophia University.

Yang Huandian. 1990. Concerning the development of the tense-lax vowel contrast in the Naxi language. Unpublished manuscript.

Yip, Moira. 1980. The tonal phonology of Chinese. Ph.D. dissertation. Massachusetts Institute of Technology. Distributed by Indiana University Linguistics Club. Published 1990. New York: Garland Press.

———. 1989. Contour tones. Phonology 6(1):149–74.

———. 1993. Tonal register in East Asian languages. In Harry van der Hulst and Keith Snider (eds.), The phonology of tone: The representation of tonal register. Linguistic Models 17:245–68. Berlin: Mouton de Gruyter.

———. 1995. Tone in East Asian languages. In John A. Goldsmith (ed.), The handbook of phonological theory, 476–94. Cambridge, Mass.: Blackwell.

Zec, Draga. 1994. Sonority constraints on prosodic structure. New York: Garland.

———. 1995. Sonority constraints on syllable structure. Phonology 12:85–130.

Zee, Eric and Ian Maddieson. 1979. Tones and tone sandhi in Shanghai: Phonetic evidence and phonological analysis. UCLA Working Papers in Phonetics 45:93–129.

www.ingramcontent.com/pod-product-compliance
Lightning Source LLC
Chambersburg PA
CBHW060955230426
43665CB00015B/2213